Terrific Training Materials

High Impact Graphic Designs
for Workbooks, Handouts, Instructor Guides,
and Job Aids

Darlene Frank

Published by

HRD Press
22 Amherst Road
Amherst, MA 01002
800-822-2801

50 South Ninth Street
Minneapolis, MN 55402
800-707-7769

First Edition, Third Printing,

Copyright © 1996 by Darlene Frank

ISBN 0-87425-315-2

Book design by Darlene Frank, Heather Havrilesky, and Elizabeth Swenson

Cover design by Eileen Klockars

Editing services by Mary George

Manufactured in Canada

To Roger Addison, who first
encouraged me to put pictures
in training materials

CONTENTS

ACKNOWLEDGMENTS

For rewording, reworking designs, and just plain working hard, Heather Havrilesky in my office earned my gratitude many times over during the writing and production of this book. Her talents and sense of humor (she wrote the Knowing Everything text) helped to make this book what it is. A special thanks also goes to Elizabeth Swenson, book designer and sculptor of the printed page.

I am grateful to those among my associates who over the years haved helped to create many successful page designs, especially Michael O'Leary, Paul Takeuchi, and Kausar Wildman. Thanks to everyone who responded to my call for examples to show in this book, and to those who sent me more research data than I had time to read.

Many thanks to the instructional design, graphic design, and technical writing experts who reviewed the draft of this book and provided the feedback that made the quality of this final version possible: Roger Addison, Carol Haig, Leslie Heyden, Lynn Kearny, Carol Malady, Bay Manning, Marna Owen, Jim Sullivan, Vince Swanson, and Kausar Wildman. And to the many friends and colleagues who expressed interest and enthusiasm during the writing process: Thank you so much — every word of encouragement meant something special to me.

PREFACE

I was in first grade. It was the last day of school. Mrs. Detweiler, my teacher, walked to the supply cabinet, opened the doors, and said, "I have some workbooks left over from this year. Would anyone like them?" My hand flew up. I don't remember if any of my classmates were interested, but I *wanted* those workbooks. She gave me three.

I felt such a thrill opening the books. Smooth, clean paper; rows of neat black print; plenty of blank lines to write on. They were objects of beauty. And they were mine. I carried them home, proud and excited.

The seed for this book must have been planted on that day. I still feel excitement turning the pages of a beautifully designed workbook, and I am fortunate enough to own a business where my associates and I produce a 1990's version of such workbooks, as well as other training materials, for business and government organizations. Along with our reputation for clear writing, we are known for producing pages that are easy to read and visually appealing.

Although something in my nature makes me appreciate beautiful pages, only education and experience have taught me the value of developing attractive printed training materials. This book is an effort to share what I have learned in a way that can benefit you and the people who use your materials. Even if you believe you have no aesthetic sense or artistic talent, this book can help you create beautiful pages.

Darlene Frank
San Francisco, CA
May 1995

INTRODUCTION

You remember the assignment: "Read chapters 6 to 9 for homework. You'll have a quiz tomorrow." You either ignored the assignment and took your chances on passing the quiz, or you read the chapters. But did you read eagerly? Did the textbooks interest you? Probably not.

Like their counterparts in high school and college, job-related training materials have a reputation for being dull. Tell someone at a party that you design training materials as part of your job, and they picture thick manuals and page after page of uninviting text.

As training professionals we have an opportunity to give people something they have received too little of by the time they reach our organizations — learning experiences that excite and inspire. This includes giving learners materials that stimulate their interest and that they enjoy using.

This book focuses on one aspect of the learning experience that has been largely absent from the handbooks of our profession — how to use graphic design principles to make printed training materials more effective. Trainers have long acknowledged the value of instructional design principles. But graphic design? Isn't that for artists?

Why graphic design is important

There are three reasons why graphic design is important in training materials:

- **Workbooks, handouts, job aids, and instructor guides are communication tools.** Their purpose is to communicate ideas and information effectively so that people learn what they need to know. Good graphic design helps achieve this goal — it motivates people to read and use the materials, it helps them learn the information more quickly, and it helps them remember more of what they learned.

- **Well-designed materials enhance your business and professional image.** The members of your audience, whether they are your employees completing a course workbook at home or a group of your peers seated before you at a conference, form an impression of you and judge the value of your information based in part on how it looks on the page. Attractive, well-designed pages are perceived as more important, and you are perceived as more credible.

- **Users of our training materials are accustomed to seeing information presented in a visually dynamic way.** Magazine ads often consist of big pictures and a few words. News stories are summarized in bullet points on the TV screen. *USA Today*'s color pictures and graphics have won it a wide audience.

  Information in our society has become increasingly visual, and print is not the preferred media of the generation raised on video games and MTV. If printed training materials don't look interesting, users are less likely to pay attention.

The *visual* aspect of communicating information has never been so important. Well-organized, clearly written content by itself is not enough — the picture that the information forms on the page is an integral part of communicating the message.

What this book will do for you

This book will show you, through dozens of examples, how to add visual interest and impact to your training materials. You don't need a graphic design background, and you don't have to create page designs that are original, trendy, or complex. What you need are rules of thumb, guidelines, and lots of not-too-complicated examples to be inspired by or to copy directly. With this book and your desktop publishing software, you can create attractive, well-designed pages.

Whether you manage a training department, work as an independent consultant, or make occasional presentations at meetings or conferences, this is a book you can turn to repeatedly for fresh ideas, answers to your questions, and specific tips on layout and design.

The result? When you distribute your handouts to seminar participants, they won't be turned off because the pages look hard to read. When your employees receive the new self-study package you spent thousands of dollars developing, they won't feel overwhelmed or disinterested because the workbooks look intimidating or bland.

Instead, people will be impressed by how professional your materials look. They will learn what they need to know more easily and quickly, and they will be much more likely to remember it. Quality materials help deliver quality training.

An added benefit of this book is that the principles and examples presented here will prove useful whenever you want to communicate information, whether you are writing procedures manuals, reports, or proposals, creating a flyer to promote a seminar, or designing screens for CBT or multimedia training. Applying graphic design principles enhances communication and learning.

How this book is organized

This book has three parts:

- **Part I** introduces four key design concepts, then devotes one chapter to each of the following graphic design elements, with examples and guidelines for using them:

    - Type
    - Lines
    - Boxes
    - Shading
    - Graphics

- **Part II** shows selected pages from training materials being used successfully by organizations and consultants, with comments and layout specifications so you can create the same look. You can duplicate the examples exactly or vary them to suit your subject and audience needs. All the examples can be produced using widely available desktop publishing software programs.

- **Part III,** the Appendixes, provides checklists and resource information.

Software you need

To create examples like those shown in this book, you will need at least a word processing program, preferably a powerful one like

Microsoft Word or WordPerfect. Many of the examples were created with other kinds of software programs, but these programs are not essential in order to produce good-looking materials.

If you want to expand your options by using a wider range of desktop publishing tools, you can benefit from the following kinds of programs in addition to a word processing program:

Software	What it does	Examples
Page layout program	Gives you more features and more control over layout and design than a word processing program	PageMaker, QuarkXPress, Ventura Publisher, FrameMaker
Illustration program	Provides tools for creating illustrations and graphics	The graphics application within Word or WordPerfect; or a separate program like MacDraw, FreeHand, Illustrator, CorelDRAW!; or Canvas
Presentation program	Creates overhead transparencies, slides, charts, and graphs	PowerPoint, Persuasion
Clip art	Provides copyright-free graphics to insert directly into your documents	Dozens of images (such as ClickArt or Mini Pics) available on disk or CD-ROM, from an online source, or packaged with an illustration or presentation program

Many of the above programs are available for both Macintosh and DOS-based computers. You will of course need a laser printer for the best results, and enough memory to run the programs. The software package or a call to the seller will let you know how much memory your system needs.

Note: This book does not explain how to use these software programs to do things like draw lines, shade part of a page, or place clip art in a document; the user manuals and other computer books can help you learn these technical skills.

Also, this book assumes that your training materials are printed in black and white.

How to use this book

This is a sourcebook of ideas and examples. It is not meant to be read from beginning to end. I suggest you read Chapter 1, which provides important background information that will help you understand and use the examples. After that, you can read whatever interests you.

You may want to thumb through the chapters or study the index to get a sense of what's here. Mark the examples you like most. Share the book with your desktop publishing staff (should you be so fortunate as to have one). Then, whenever you need inspiration or ideas to use in your materials, look for an example among these pages.

By using this book you will not only improve your page design skills, you will also become familiar with graphic design terminology and the issues involved in laying out pages. Familiarity with these issues will help you communicate with a graphic designer, your manager, or your production staff. This book can help you express more clearly and specifically exactly how you want your materials to look.

Using the examples

Here are some ideas on how to use the examples:

- **When you find a page layout you like, copy it.** Put your information into the same format. This is what graphic designers do. Your page will look somewhat different because your information is different, but the layout you like will still be there. You may not be able to duplicate an example exactly, due to differences in your software, fonts, or printing process, but you can come close.

- **Create your own designs** based on what you see here. Notice what you like and don't like about the examples. Once you've learned how the graphic design elements can be used, you will find many ways of combining them on your own. Keep your designs simple — the trick is to combine elements without creating a busy page.

- **Supplement the ideas in this book** with examples from other sources. Look for ideas everywhere. Keep a file of designs you like. Some of my favorite ideas on file are a 1955 French-language job aid, a flyer for the West German lottery, magazine ads, and newsletters from utility companies.

  Sources like these can help you keep your materials looking fresh and current. Just keep your audience in mind at all times. Huge titles and paragraphs of tiny print may look striking in a sports car ad, but will they contribute to learning for your audience?

Things to keep in mind

Here are a few things to keep in mind as you use this book:

- **Pretty pages are of little value if your materials are poorly written**, poorly organized, or not based on sound instructional design. Your goal should be total quality; don't neglect any one aspect in favor of another.

- **There is no one correct graphic design technique** in any situation, just traditions and rules of thumb that have evolved since the first printing press. Graphic designers do not always agree on what is best, and personal likes and dislikes play a role in designing almost any page.

- **You're the training expert**, and decisions about the design of your materials are ultimately yours. You may decide to ignore a graphic design guideline because you believe doing so is in the best interests of your audience. Time constraints may lead you to sacrifice some visual appeal to meet a deadline or to make revisions easier, and sometimes you'll have to make your materials consistent in format with others that are poorly designed.

- **Training materials do not have to win graphic design awards** to be effective. They just need to be inviting and appropriate for your particular audience. Most of the examples in this book were created not by graphic designers but by training professionals who have an eye for layout or an interest in page design. They have found that the more they apply graphic design principles, the more professionally produced their materials look, and the more favorable the response from users.

Whether your goal is to design a single worksheet or a 200-page instructor guide, you will find this book a rich source of examples and ideas that will stimulate creative ideas of your own. Your training materials can look terrific.

I

Graphic Design Elements

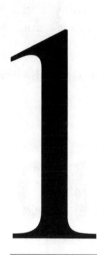

FOUR DESIGN BASICS

In graphic design books you will find a discussion of design principles such as unity, harmony, balance, coherence, conflict, rhythm, dominance, and more. Unless you plan to study graphic design in depth, reading about these abstract concepts won't do much to improve the look of your training materials.

Taking a more practical approach, Robin Williams, in *The Non-Designer's Design Book*, has identified just four principles that people without a design background can benefit from the most:

- Contrast

- Repetition

- Proximity

- Alignment

By learning about these four principles and noticing how they are applied throughout this book, you will be able to start producing better-looking materials immediately. This chapter explains the principles.

Contrast

Contrast is created by juxtaposing elements that are very different — large and small, black and white, wide and narrow, thick and thin. On a page with low contrast, the elements look much the same; nothing jumps out, and the overall "color" of the page often looks gray.

A page with high contrast appears stronger, bolder, more dynamic, and more interesting. Important elements, like headings and symbols, stand out clearly and are easy to find. Although a low-contrast page is sometimes appropriate (maybe in a financial report), training materials will be easier to use and more appealing to readers if they have high contrast.

Here are some easy ways to create contrast on the page.

Use **large and small type** together.

Use **one large graphic** on a page, or use a large and small graphic together.

Use **black and white,** or **black and light shading,** together.

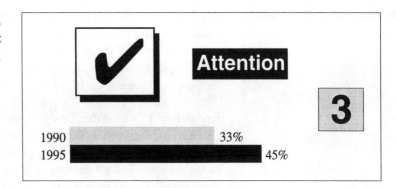

Use **heavy and light lines** on the same page.

Learning Everything In One Lesson

Leave plenty of **white space** and make the **headings large and bold.** White space lightens the page and makes it more inviting. Don't be afraid to use it.

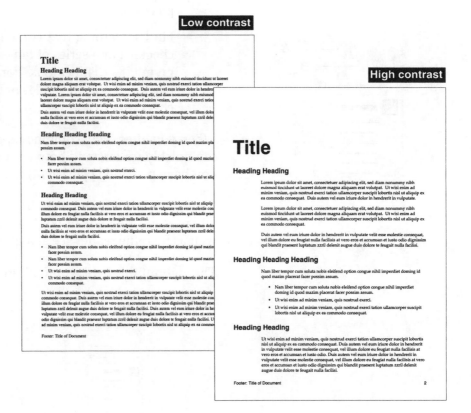

You will find more about contrast and many other examples of it throughout this book.

Repetition

Repetition is created in part by being consistent. Developers of training materials are good at consistency — they usually put section titles in the same place on each title page, give each level of heading its own style, include the same information in all the footers, and more. Trainers know that consistency helps learners.

Repetition in a graphic design sense means deliberately repeating a visual element to add interest to your pages and to help unify the entire document. Consistently repeating something in the same way makes all the pages look like they belong to the same document. Repetition throughout a series of documents can make each piece look like part of the same "family."

Here are some examples of how you might create repetition:

- Put a bold line under every major heading.

- Turn the page number into a graphic.

- Repeat an element from the cover inside the document. For example, if a logo has a triangle or bold lines in it, repeat the triangle or lines in the document.

- Repeat an illustration in different sizes, or repeat small pieces of it.

- Find something that you have repeated anyway, like a checklist or a series of tables, then make it stronger by giving it a distinct look. For example, use reverse (white on black) titles in the tables or big, bold numbers in the checklists.

More page number ideas on page 61.

When you effectively combine repetition with contrast, readers can quickly understand how your materials are organized because you have provided consistent, noticeable visual cues.

Repetition is important even in a one-page handout or job aid, where a repeated line or bold heading can create visual interest as well as help the reader see at a glance how the page is organized.

Throughout this book you will find many examples of repetition.

Proximity

Training professionals know that breaking information into small pieces like short paragraphs and bulleted lists, then grouping the related pieces into a unit, helps people understand and learn the information. Proximity refers to the *visual* grouping of related pieces, so that the page looks organized and readers can see the relationship between elements at a glance. Research has shown that elements that are visually grouped are understood more quickly.

Look at the following examples.

Visually grouping the related elements on this handout cover page helps organize the page and makes it easier to read. It also uses the white space more effectively. Notice how the white space appears broken up in the first example, more organized in the second.

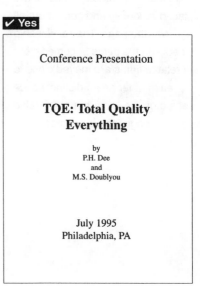

✗ No

Conference Presentation

TQE: Total Quality Everything

by

P.H. Dee

and

M.S. Doublyou

July 1995

Philadelphia, PA

✔ Yes

Conference Presentation

TQE: Total Quality Everything

by
P.H. Dee
and
M.S. Doublyou

July 1995
Philadelphia, PA

In this list the relationship between items becomes clear much more quickly when they are grouped visually. Whenever possible, group related items, and leave more space between the groups than between the items within a group.

✗ No

Account number
123-235-1548
Verify
File number
122-47-9990
Check
Activity code
1234-5655-8976-9009
Enter
Employee code
94-479875
Duplicate

✔ Yes

Account number
123-235-1548
Verify

File number
122-47-9990
Check

Activity code
1234-5655-8976-9009
Enter

Employee code
94-479875
Duplicate

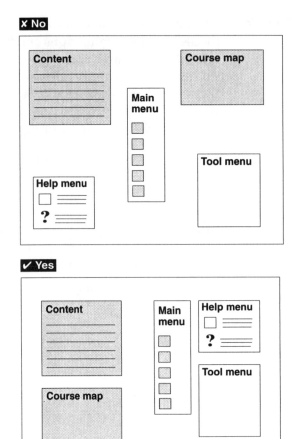

In the top example the items are placed randomly and spread out all over the page. The relationship between the items becomes clear when related items are moved close to each other and a distinct space separates the two groups. This also makes the page look more organized.

Ideally, headings should be placed closer to the text that follows them than to the text that precedes them. **The rule of thumb is twice as much space above as below.** Leaving more space above indicates visually which block of text the heading relates to, and helps the reader.

To achieve this result, you may want to use the paragraph spacing (space before and after) feature in your word processing or page layout program. Getting the spacing right may require some trial and error.

✗ No

diam nonummy nibh euismod tincidunt ut.

Heading

Lorem ipsum dolor sit amet, consectetuer adipiscing elit, sed diam nonummy nibh euismod.

Heading

Lorem ipsum dolor sit amet, consectetuer adipiscing elit, sed diam nonummy nibh euismod tincidunt ut loreet dolore.

Heading

Lorem ipsum dolor sit amet, consectetuer adipiscing elit, sed diam nonummy nibh euismod

✔ Yes

diam nonummy nibh euismod tincidunt ut.

Heading

Lorem ipsum dolor sit amet, consectetuer adipiscing elit, sed diam nonummy nibh euismod.

Heading

Lorem ipsum dolor sit amet, consectetuer adipiscing elit, sed diam nonummy nibh euismod tincidunt ut loreet dolore.

Heading

Lorem ipsum dolor sit amet, consectetuer adipiscing elit, sed

Alignment

Like proximity, alignment helps to organize the page. It creates order. You create alignment by lining up the edges of the elements on a page. Whenever possible, align everything on the page with something else on the page. Look at the two pages below.

Look at the edges of the elements on this page. Notice how many items do not line up with anything else.

✗ No

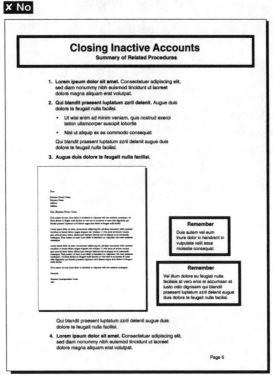

✔ Yes

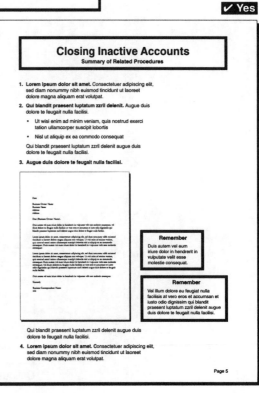

Here the elements are aligned along the left, right, and bottom edges. The page looks more orderly and inviting, and the design is stronger. Although you may have to train your eye to notice these alignments, it's worth it — subtle touches like these help to give your documents a professional look.

Aligning text

Creating alignment also includes deciding how to align the text on a page. You have four options:

- Left aligned (more commonly called flush left, ragged right, or unjustified)

- Right aligned

- Justified

- Centered

Educational research favors the use of flush left/ragged right text. Readers slow down (as much as 10 percent) when reading justified text.

This is **flush left** (or **left aligned, ragged right,** or **unjustified**) text. It is easier to read because type is naturally spaced (the space between words is equal). It is informal, widely used, and familiar to readers. And it adds white space at the ends of lines.

This is **justified** text. It is more formal and almost always requires hyphenation (which impedes reading). It also creates unnatural space between words and letters (making text harder to read). It should not be used in narrow columns of text.

This is **right aligned** text. It is useful for labels and callouts placed to the left of a figure or illustration (as in this book), for headings placed in the left margin, and for title and cover pages.

Three uses for right aligned text.

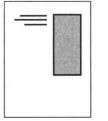

Callouts

Headings in the left margin

Title pages

This is **centered** text. Trainers use it a lot; graphic designers don't. A left or right alignment is stronger, more interesting, and more sophisticated.

This cover page looks cleaner and more sophisticated when all the elements are aligned along the left edge. Making the bold lines equal in length creates an alignment along the right edge as well.

✗ No

Conference Presentation

TQE: Total Quality Everything

by
P.H. Dee
and
M.S. Doublyou

July 1995
Philadelphia, PA

✔ Yes

Conference Presentation

TQE: Total Quality Everything
P.H. Dee & M.S. Doublyou

July 1995
Philadelphia, PA

This list looks chaotic when it's centered. When it's left-aligned, it looks stronger and more organized.

✗ No

Instructional Design
✔ Analysis
✔ Design
✔ Development
✔ Implementation
✔ Evaluation

✔ Yes

Instructional Design
✔ Analysis
✔ Design
✔ Development
✔ Implementation
✔ Evaluation

When the text is flush left, don't center the headings above it. The alignment is stronger and the page looks better when the headings are flush left as well.

✗ No

✔ Yes

Applying the four principles

When you effectively apply the principles of contrast, repetition, proximity, and alignment, each page becomes a "picture" that looks good and helps the reader as well. Contrast makes important elements stand out and draws the reader in; repetition adds visual interest and consistency. Proximity and alignment make the relationship between elements clear, and organize the page. All four principles make your materials more attractive and more effective learning and communication tools.

As you look at the examples in this book, notice what gives a page contrast, what design elements are repeated, how the elements are grouped, and where things are aligned. Printed pages are likely to look different to you from now on, because you will see them in light of these principles. And your training materials will look different (and better) as well, as you apply these principles.

The remaining chapters in this section provide guidelines and rules of thumb for using specific graphic design elements: type, lines, boxes, shading, and graphics.

SUMMARY of the four principles

- Create pages with high contrast.

- Leave plenty of white space.

- Deliberately repeat a graphic design element throughout a document.

- Do not spread things out all over the page or place things randomly on the page. Put related items close to each other, and leave more space between the groups of items than between the individual items.

- Place headings closer to the text that follows them than to the text that precedes them.

- Align the edges of things. Line everything up with something else on the page.

- Avoid centered alignments.

2 TYPE

Type is the most basic graphic design element you'll use in designing pages. The typeface you choose, how large or small you make the letters, and how you space the words on the page can either help or hinder learners. Even if your typeface choices are limited, and even if you don't use other design elements such as lines or shading, your materials can still look well-designed if you use type effectively.

This chapter provides guidelines and rules of thumb for using type to make your pages inviting and readable.

To begin, let's clarify the difference between the words *typeface* and *font*.

Times	Times is a typeface.
Times Bold *Times Italic* ***Times Bold Italic***	These are fonts. Fonts are individual members of a typeface family.

Most of the time I'll use the word *typeface* because I am referring to a complete type family, including all of its fonts.

Categories of type

This chart shows three broad categories of type you should be familiar with, and gives guidelines for their use.

	Examples	Guidelines for use
# serif Serifs are like small feet.	Bookman New Century Schoolbook Palatino Times	• Use serif for long lines or long blocks of text. • Use serif if learners have reading difficulties or impaired vision. • You can also use serif for anything listed in the sans serif category.

## sans serif 	
 	
"Sans" means without. Thus, no serifs.
	Avant Garde
	
	Helvetica
	
	Helvetica Condensed
		• Sans serif is best used for short lines or short blocks of text.
		• Sans serif is widely used for:
		  – titles and headings
		  – captions and labels
		  – tables and lists

script Script looks handwritten.	**Dom Casual** Tekton	• Use script only in very small amounts or very short blocks of text. It is hard to read. • Script looks good in large point sizes. • Don't use all caps.

Choosing a typeface

Choosing a typeface is more a matter of personal preference than of following rules. Each typeface has its own characteristics, and people respond to them differently. One person will describe Times as familiar, another as conservative and overused. One will describe Bookman as strong and readable, another as elementary and schoolbookish. Follow these two guidelines:

- Use a typeface that is legible given the paper and printing process you will use. New Century Schoolbook, for example, is legible even when print quality is poor.

- Use a typeface that is appropriate for your purpose and audience. For example, if the participants in your seminar are likely to perceive Bookman as too unsophisticated, use another typeface.

Which is better: serif or sans serif?

Most of us find serif type easier to read because we have grown up reading it and are used to it. Also, the tiny serifs help to guide the eye horizontally across the page.

Although studies have shown that sans serif type in short lines is just as legible as serif, most experts agree that serif is the better choice for large amounts of text, especially if people are required to read it. Research has also shown that readers seem to prefer serif type.

The use of sans serif has increased in recent years, and people have grown more accustomed to reading it. It's possible that some people in your training audience may even prefer it. If you want to use sans serif in large amounts, it's best to test it on your readers.

Avoid these fonts and type styles in training materials. Zapf Chancery is a particularly hard-to-read script. These city-name fonts are of the early desktop publishing variety; so many other fonts are now available that look more professional. Outline and shadow lettering are hard to read and look amateurish.

Fonts and type styles to avoid

Zapf Chancery

Chicago, Geneva
Monaco, New York

Outline lettering

Shadow lettering

Combining typefaces

Developers of training materials often ask, "What are the rules for combining typefaces?" Here they are:

- **Don't combine two typefaces from the same type category on one page.** For example, don't use two serifs (like Times and Palatino) on the same page; don't use two sans serifs (like Helvetica and Avant Garde) on the same page.

  The purpose of combining typefaces is to create contrast, and typefaces in the same category look too much alike. (Graphic designers can break this rule, but only because they understand the subtle differences between typefaces.)

- **The only effective combination is a serif and a sans serif.** Use a serif typeface for the main text, and a sans serif for titles and headings (and possibly for headers, footers, captions, and callouts as well). Or vice versa.

- **Don't combine script with any other typeface.** That means if you use Tekton or Dom Casual, use it alone on the page. Don't combine it with Times, Palatino, Helvetica, or anything else.

- **Don't use more than two typefaces on a page**, or more than five in a document.

- **If you are using only one typeface:**
  - Make the headings and titles large and bold enough to create contrast.
  - Create variety by using bold, italics, and different sizes of type.

A graphic design technique for creating contrast is to use a heavy, black sans serif font like one of these for headings, and a lightweight typeface for text. If you use just one font like this, you can enhance your pages dramatically. See examples on pages 72, 74, 86, and 110.

Franklin Gothic Heavy

Gill Sans Extra Bold

Helvetica Black

Univers Black

Point size

Type

is measured in points, from the top of the tallest letter to the bottom of the longest. There are 72 points to an inch.

See page 88 for guidelines for overhead transparencies.

The most important criteria in determining point size is legibility: Will your audience be able to read your materials easily, given the paper you'll print on and the conditions under which they will be used? If you're printing a set of handouts on beige parchment paper, small type will not be easy to read. Pages that will be viewed close up can be printed in smaller type than pages that will be read from across a desk.

As you can see by looking at the bottom of this page, typefaces vary in size. You need to choose a typeface first, then determine point size.

RULES OF THUMB

- Use 10- to 14-point type for the main text (also called *body text*) in workbooks and handouts. Don't use 14-point just because it's large; use it only for a good reason. For example, some readers over 40 may prefer large type.

- Type can be as small as 8 points in tables and job aids, captions and callouts, headers and footers.

- Where content is not critical, such as in copyright notices or certain parts of headers and footers, type can be smaller than 8 points, as long as it is legible in the final printed materials.

- Use smaller type in narrow columns, larger type in wide columns.

- Use no more than three point sizes per page, five per document.

- When you're not sure if type will be legible, make it larger.

Even in the same point size, typefaces take up different amounts of space.

Helvetica Condensed	This is 12-point type and we are running out of space. What will we do abo
Times	This is 12-point type and we are running out of space. What will we do ab
Helvetica	This is 12-point type and we are running out of space. What will we
Palatino	This is 12-point type and we are running out of space. What will w
New Century Schoolbook	This is 12-point type and we are running out of space. What will
Avant Garde	This is 12-point type and we are running out of space. What w
Bookman	This is 12-point type and we are running out of space. What

Leading

The amount of space between lines of type is called *leading* (rhymes with *heading*). Leading is measured in points, just like type. Default (automatic) leading is usually 120 percent of the point size of the type. For example, 10-point type will have 12 points of leading.

Too little space between lines of type makes them hard to read. In a page layout program you can increase or decrease the space between lines by adjusting the leading. In a word processing program you adjust the space between lines by using single, one and one-half, or double spacing, although some programs allow you to adjust the leading as well.

The default leading will work just fine in most cases.

12-point type/10-point leading

Lorem ipsum dolor sit. Lorem ipsum dolor sit. Lorem ipsum dolor sit. Lorem ipsum dolor sit. Lorem ipsum dolor sit.

12-point type/Default leading

Lorem ipsum dolor sit. Lorem ipsum dolor sit. Lorem ipsum dolor sit. Lorem ipsum dolor sit. Lorem ipsum dolor sit.

12-point type/18-point leading

Lorem ipsum dolor sit. Lorem ipsum dolor sit. Lorem ipsum dolor sit. Lorem ipsum dolor sit. Lorem ipsum dolor sit.

RULES OF THUMB

- As line length increases, the need for leading increases also; wide columns or long lines of type are easier to read when they have more space between them.

- Sans serif used in long lines of text needs more leading than serif.

- When in doubt, use more leading.

Line length

How long should you make a line of text? As a rule of thumb, 40 to 60 characters per line facilitates reading and comprehension. There are other measures, such as eight to ten words of average length, or four to five inches.

You need to take into account the subject matter, typeface, point size, and amount of space between the lines, as shown in the examples below.

Since typefaces vary in size, you can try typing one and one-half to two lower-case alphabets (39 to 52 characters) in the typeface and point size you'll be using. In the 11-point Palatino you're reading, a 52-character line length looks like this and is about four inches long:

abcdefghijklmnopqrstuvwxyzabcdefghijklmnopqrstuvwxyz

If you're unsure how long the line should be, shorter is usually better.

Long lines of text

You can use **long** lines of text if:

- The typeface is highly legible
- The point size is large
- There is a lot of space between the lines
- The content is smooth narrative that requires little study

Alice and Patricia have worked together for 14 years. Six months ago, Alice and Patricia both applied for the position of unit supervisor. Alice got the job. Last weekend, Patricia worked on Saturday and was responsible for locking up. On Monday morning,

Short lines of text

Use **short** lines of text if:

- The type is small
- There is not much space between the lines
- The content is complex or technical

Calculating the calibration between the x and y points will require using three directional median and four conversion point formulas. Although most engineering experiments with this tool have resulted in similar or

Tabs and indents

Here are a few examples of how to use tabs and indents.

Using the default tab setting often results in large gaps between numbers or bullets and the text next to them. Manually set a tab to avoid large gaps.

✗ No

1.	Who did it?
2.	What was done?
3.	When did it happen?
4.	Why did they do it?

✔ Yes

1.	Who did it?
2.	What was done?
3.	When did it happen?
4.	Why did they do it?

Don't indent the first line of a paragraph if you have put space between the paragraphs. Either one indicates the start of a new paragraph; using both is unnecessary.

✗ No

Heading

Lorem ipsum dolorsit amet, consectetuer adipiscing elit, sed diam nonummy nibh euismod tincidunt ut laoreet.

Ut wisi enim ad minim veniam, quis nostrud exerci tation ullamcorper suscipit lobortis nis ut aliquip.

Lorem ipsum dolorsit amet, consectetuer adipiscing elit, sed diam nonummy nibh euismod

✔ Yes

Heading

Lorem ipsum dolorsit amet, consectetuer adipiscing elit, sed diam nonummy nibh euismod tincidunt ut laoreet.

Ut wisi enim ad minim veniam, quis nostrud exerci tation ullamcorper suscipit lobortis nis ut aliquip ex.

Lorem ipsum dolorsit amet, consectetuer adipiscing elit, sed diam nonummy nibh euismod

Wide tab settings between columns make this list difficult to read. Adjust the tabs to make reading easier; don't spread things out just because the space is available.

✗ No

Installation time	2-3 wks
Direct transfer	24-48 hrs
Turnaround	4-48 hrs
–PC	1 day
–Fax/phone	1/2 day
–Paper	2 days
Errors corrected	1 day

✔ Yes

Installation time	2-3 wks
Direct transfer	24-48 hrs
Turnaround	4-48 hrs
–PC	1 day
–Fax/phone	1/2 day
–Paper	2 days
Errors corrected	1 day

Headings and titles

Headings and titles guide the reader through a document and indicate the hierarchy of information. Levels of headings are usually differentiated by size, type style, position, space around them, a symbol, or some combination of these.

Words in all caps all have a similar rectangular shape, therefore readers must work harder to recognize them. Words not in all caps have varying shapes due to the ascenders and descenders (the parts of the letters that extend above and below the line), making them easier to recognize. Also, words in all caps take up more space.

RULES OF THUMB

- Avoid using ALL CAPS except in very short titles and headings. All caps are hard to read.

LEARNING EVERYTHING IN ONE WORKSHOP

Learning Everything in One Workshop

- Consider capitalizing only the first word of a title or heading. Capitalizing all or most words is a habit left over from newspaper typesetting practices and, some graphic designers argue, is unnecessary and presents words in an unnatural style. In this book I have capitalized only the first word in headings because I think it looks simpler and is easier to read.

- Don't hyphenate titles.

- Break lines at a verbal pause.

✗ No	✔ Yes
Trainers Who Train Too Much Need A Break	**Trainers Who Train Too Much Need A Break**

- Don't put a heading by itself at the bottom of a page; put at least two lines of text after it.

- Don't use more than three levels of headings; more are harder for readers to keep track of. Make each level visually distinct.

Level 1	■ Level 1	■ Level 1	Level 1
Level 2	■ Level 2	• Level 2	Level 2
Level 3	• Level 3	*Level 3*	Level 3

Creating emphasis

There are four traditional ways of using type to emphasize important words:

- *Italics*
- **Bold**
- ***Bold italics***
- <u>Underlining</u>

These three are referred to as type style. Type not emphasized in one of these ways is called *normal*.

Training materials use a lot of emphasis, and the text often ends up looking like this:

> ***<u>THREE LINES OR MORE OF BOLDFACE, PLUS ITALICS, PLUS UNDERLINING, PLUS ALL CAPS AS WELL, TO MAKE SURE NO ONE MISSES THE MESSAGE.</u>***

It's easy to emphasize things this way, but it's not good graphic design. Large amounts of text in italics or boldface are hard to read. Underlining is reminiscent of typewriters, and cuts through letters that descend below the line. Minimize its use, unless your page layout program allows you to drop the underline so that it is lower than the descenders, like this:

Please <u>sign up</u>

Consider the following alternatives for creating emphasis.

Use **larger type.** In a word processing program, this may create uneven spacing between lines of text.

We want to emphasize strongly that this is **really important** and you should always remember it.

Use a **contrasting typeface.** Here the bold sans serif catches your eye. You may have to make the sans serif type one point size smaller to avoid extra space between the lines.

We want to emphasize strongly that this is **really important** and you should always remember it.

Change the **line length,** usually by indenting one or both sides. This puts white space around the emphasized text. The vertical line added here also draws attention to the indented text.

We want to emphasize strongly that this is really important and you should always remember it. We want to emphasize strongly that

> this is really important
> and you should always
> remember it. We want to
> emphasize strongly that
> this is really important
> and you should always
> remember it.

We want to emphasize strongly that this is really important and you should always remember it. We want to emphasize strongly that this is important.

Use **reverse type** (white on black). To make sure reverse type will be legible, use a bold sans serif typeface (unless the type is very large). Always use reverse type in small amounts; large amounts are hard to read.

We want to emphasize strongly that this is **really important** and you should always remember it.

In other chapters you will find examples of how to use boxes and shading for emphasis.

Variety

Try the following to create variety with type.

Expand or condense headings. You will get the best results with a page layout program; a word processing program may do this, but it may not look the way you'd like.

Heading Heading Condensed, width set at 70%

Heading Heading Normal

Heading Heading Expanded, width set at 130%

Use **bullets and dingbats** (ornamental characters) to add contrast. Don't use asterisks in list items (they went out with typewriters).

- List item
- List item
- List item

◆ List item
◆ List item
◆ List item

▶ List item
▶ List item
▶ List item

Dingbats ✦ ■ ▲ ▼ ✓ ★ ❏ ➤ ☞

Put the **first line** of a chapter or section in all **capital letters**.

IN THE BEGINNING NO ONE THOUGHT training was important. Then they began to hear stories of remarkable things that had happened in other lands.

Use **small caps.** Remember that words in all caps are hard to read; use them only in short titles and headings.

USE ONLY IN SHORT TITLES

Use a **large initial capital letter.** Use these sparingly (one per column, two per page). Don't make them larger than the capital letters in the title. Notice where the large letter is aligned with the text in each example.

Dolor sit. Lorem ipsum dolor sit amet, consectetuer adipiscing elit, sed diam nonummy nibh euismod tincidunt ut laoreet dolore magna aliquam erat volutpat. Ut wisi enim ad minim veniam, quis nostrud exerci tation ullamcorper suscipit lobortis.

Dolor sit. Lorem ipsum dolor sit amet, consectetuer adipiscing elit, sed diam nonummy nibh euismod tincidunt ut laoreet dolore magna aliquam erat volutpat. Ut wisi enim ad minim veniam, quis nostrud exerci tation ullamcorper suscipit lobortis.

Use a **bleed.** A bleed is anything that prints off the edge of the paper. Bleeds cost more to print because the paper has to be trimmed. Also, unless your laser printer can handle 11-by-17-inch paper, you won't be able to see exactly what the finished product will look like until it comes back from your commercial printer.

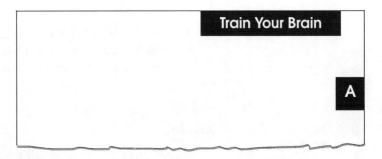

Train Your Brain

A

A professionally typeset look

Here are a few tips that will help make your materials look professionally typeset.

Quotation marks

- Use true quotation marks, sometimes called *smart* quotes or *curly* quotes, and apostrophes (" ' ' "). Straight quotes (") (') were the only ones available on typewriters.

Hyphens and dashes

- Use a hyphen (-) only to hyphenate words. Limit hyphenation; too much interferes with reading.

- Use an en dash (–), not a hyphen (-):

    – as a substitute for the word *to* between numbers that indicate duration or a range

    – as a minus sign

    10:30–11:00; June 6–12; pages 55–59

    30 – 20 = 10

    Many publishers put a small space before and after the en dash. The space is necessary only with a minus sign.

- Use an em dash (—), not two hyphens (--), as a break in thought. No space is necessary before or after it.

Spacing

- Put one space, not two, after punctuation at the end of a sentence. Typewriters required two; desktop publishing requires only one.

- Always put some space between a bullet and the text to the right of it.

- Create a fill-in-the-blank (_____) by using the tab key or space bar along with the underlining feature. Don't use the underscore key because it may print like this (_ _ _ _ _ _).

Not kerned   Kerned

To To

Kerning is used most often to move a lower case a, e, o, r, u, or w closer to an upper case W, Y, T, or P.

Kerning

- Kerning is a way of adjusting the space between individual letters. It is used most often to reduce the space between certain pairs of letters in titles that are printed in very large type. Some word processing programs do not provide a kerning option. You will rarely need it anyway.

3

LINES

Lines (also called *rules* by graphic designers) are one of the simplest yet most useful design elements. Look at almost any sophisticated page design, and you will find one or more lines used to separate, emphasize, or define.

Developers of training materials use lines primarily to separate text, such as a line between blocks of information, or a line between the header or footer and the rest of the page.

Regardless of how you use a line, you should think of it as a graphic design element, and make a conscious decision about:

- How thick to make it
- What to align it with
- How much space to leave around it
- Where to repeat it

Use lines deliberately, and think of them as an important part of the overall design of the page.

This chapter shows examples of lines used in a variety of ways.

Examples of lines

Lines can be created in different point sizes. The thickness of a line is referred to as line "weight." Some word processing programs do not provide many line weight options; you may be limited to "hairline," "single," or "thick." The lines in this box were created in PageMaker.

Use broken lines with caution — they can make a page look busy.

Line Varieties

————————————	Hairline
————————————	1 pt.
————————————	2 pt.
————————————	6 pt.

GUIDELINES for using lines

- Horizontal lines are inviting; too many vertical lines create a busy page.

- Light lines generally look better than heavy lines, especially if there are many lines on the page.

- Put more space around heavy lines.

- Don't use too many different line lengths on one page.

- Don't place text too close to a line.

All About Everything

Introduction

The only way to know everything about everything is to learn about it in a self-study. The only way to know almost everything about everything is to learn about it in a self-study. The only way to know everything about everything is definitely to learn about it in a self-study.

The only way to know everything about everything is to learn about it in a self-study. The only way to know everything about everything is to learn about it in a self-study. There is no other fast and friendly way to know everything. The only way to know everything about everything is to try to learn about it in a self-study. The only absolute way to know everything about everything is to learn all about it in a self-study.

The Only Way

The only way to know everything about everyth[...] only way to know everything about everything i[...]

- The only way to know everything about [...] self-study. It's the only way to know eve[...]
- The only way to know everything about [...]
- The only way to know everything about [...] study.

Know Everything

The only way to know everything about everyth[...] only way to know everything about everything i[...] no other way to know absolutely everything.

The only way to know everything about everyth[...] There is no other way to know everything. The [...] everything is to learn about it in a self-study.

The only way to know everything about everyth[...] only way to know everything about everything i[...]

The Everything Series

A thick and thin line set off the title; lighter lines separate blocks of information. Notice the light lines are aligned with the text, not with the headings.

Section 2. Knowing Everything

Introduction

Contrary to popular belief, it *is* possible to know everything. And the surprising thing is, it takes a lot less time and energy than you might think.

The first, most important step to knowing everything is remembering everything that everyone has ever told you. This doesn't take much effort. Every time you hear something you haven't heard before, commit it to memory immediately.

Contrary to popular belief, it *is* possible to know everything. And the surprising thing is, it takes a lot less time and energy than you might think.

- The first, most important step to knowing everything is remembering everything that everyone has ever told you.
- This doesn't take much effort. Every time you hear something you haven't heard before, commit it to memory immediately.
- Seco[...] you [...] deci[...] infor[...]
- Gen[...] you [...]

More Than Everything

It *is* poss[...] is, it take[...] think.

The first,[...] rememb[...] This doe[...]

Contrary[...] thing. An[...] and ener[...]

The first,[...] rememb[...]

Know It All Self-Study

A heavy line emphasizes the title; a lighter line is used in the footer.

It Is Possible to Know It All!

Contrary to popular belief, it *is* possible to know everything. And the surprising thing is, it takes a lot less time and energy than you might think.

The first, most important step to knowing everything is remembering everything that everyone has ever told you.

The Key to Knowing Everything

The first, most important step to knowing everything is remembering everything that everyone has ever told you.

This doesn't take much effort. Every time you hear something you haven't heard before, commit it to memory immediately. Second, it is very important to remember everything you read or see on T.V.

Ways of Knowing Everything

Contrary to popular belief, it *is* possible to know everything. And the surprising thing is, it takes a lot less time and energy than you might think.

The first, most important step to knowing everything is remembering everything that everyone has ever told you.

This doesn't take much effort. Every time you hear something you haven't

heard before, commit it to memory immediately. Don't forget to remember and don't ever forget. An easy rule to follow when deciding what to remember is: if it contains any information whatsoever, remember.

The first, most important step to knowing everything is remembering everything that everyone has ever told you. This doesn't take much effort.

Every time you hear something you haven't heard before, commit it to memory immediately. Second, it is very important to remember everything you read or see on T.V.

Advantages of Knowing

An easy rule to follow when deciding what to remember is: if it contains any information whatsoever, remember.

Generally, this means remembering everything. If you can just remember to do this, then knowing everything is within reach! The first, most important step to knowing everything is remembering everything that everyone has ever told you.

This doesn't take much effort. Every time you hear something you haven't heard before, commit it to memory immediately.

- A Guide To Everything
- Knowing It All: A Step By Step Guide
- More Than Enough: Knowing Too Much Is Sometimes Not The Best Idea
- A Guide To Everything
- Knowing It All: A Step By Step Guide

Knowledge Possibilities   2

Bold lines separate sections of information. Putting the lines above, not below, the headings indicates clearly that a heading belongs with the text that follows it.

A horizontal line separates the introductory paragraphs from the rest of the page.

A vertical line separates the headings in the left column from the text on the right. A horizontal line is part of the footer.

Horizontal lines set off the column headings and separate the steps in a leader's guide.

Customer Service Reps 1

Knowledge of Everything

Background

Contrary to popular belief, it *is* possible to know everything. And the surprising thing is, it takes a lot less time and energy than you might think.

The first, most important step to knowing everything is remembering everything that everyone has ever told you. This doesn't take much effort. Every time you hear something you haven't heard before, commit it to memory immediately. Second, it is very important to remember everything you read or see on TV.

What Is Knowledge of Everything?

The first, most important step to knowing everything is remembering everything that everyone has ever told you. This doesn't take much effort.

Every time you hear something you haven't heard before, commit it to memory immediately. Second, it is very important to remember everything you read or see on TV:

- Try to remember absolutely everything, no matter what you do. This part is crucial.
- Keep a little book with you and write down every new fact.
- Commit everything you hear or see to memory.

Your Responsibility

The first, most important step to knowing everything is remembering everything that everyone has ever told you. This doesn't take much effort.

❗ STAY ALERT! If you spot someone who looks like they might know everything, pay attention to everything they say; you could learn a great deal from them.

What Is Knowledge of Everything?

The first, most important step to knowing everything is remembering everything that everyone has ever told you. This doesn't take much effort. Every time you hear something you haven't heard before, commit it to memory immediately. Second, it is very important to remember everything you read...

How Ca... Everyth...

The first, everythin everyone take muc somethin commit i it is very you read

Contrary know ev is, it take you migh

---

2. *Knowing Everything*

Introduction

The only way to know everything about everything is to learn about it in a self-study. The only way to know everything about everything is to learn about it in a self-study.

The only way to know everything about everything is to learn about it in a self-study. The only way to know everything about everything is to learn about it in a self-study. The only way to know everything about everything is to learn about it in a self-study.

The Only Way

The only way to know everything about everything is to learn about it in a self-study. The only way to know everything about everything is to learn about it in a self-study. The only way to know everything about everything is to learn about it in a self-study.

The only way to know everything about everything is to learn about it in a everything is know.

Know Everything

The only wa about it in a everything i know everyt study.

- The onl
- The onl
- The onl about it

Knowing Everything Self-Study

OUTLINE   **Module 3**

TIME	WORKBOOK PAGE	OUTLINE	VISUALS
ST 2:35 BL 5 min	3-11 & 3-12	10. Step 5: Produce a schedule* – Staffing schedule How to use	18 Blank Schedule 19 Graph K
		TRANSITION: You've completed a learning schedule for a standard day. Let's look at what to do with the exceptions you've discovered. You need extra hours for exception days. Ask: Where will you get them?	
ST 2:40 BL 45 min.	3-13	11. Step 5: Schedule exceptions* – Review job aid steps – Review example using graph – Summarize steps – Explain how to gain extra FTE – Check for understanding	20 Exceptions 21 Graph L
		TRANSITION: Now let's do some scheduling.	
ST 3:25 BL 15 min.		BREAK	

LEADER'S GUIDE   3-7

Finally, It Is Possible!

Contrary to popular belief, it *is* possible to know everything. And the surprising thing is, it takes a lot less time and energy than you might think.

The first, most important step to knowing everything is remembering everything that everyone has ever told you.

- What you know
- What your friends know
- What is left to know

The first, most important step to knowing everything is remembering everything that everyone has ever told you.

The Key to Knowing All

The first, most important step to knowing everything is remembering everything that everyone has ever told you.

This doesn't take much effort. Every time you hear something you haven't heard before, commit it to memory immediately. Second, it is very important to remember everything you read or see on TV.

Contrary to popular belief, it *is* possible to know everything. And the surprising thing is, it takes a lot less time and energy than you might think.

6

The first, most important step to knowing everything is remembering everything that everyone has ever told you.

The first, most important step to knowing everything is remembering everything that everyone has ever told you.

This doesn't take much effort. Every time you hear something you haven't heard before, commit it to memory immediately. Second, it is very important to remember everything you read or see on TV.

- Contrary to popular belief, it *is* possible to know everyth...
- And the surprising thing is, it takes a...
- The first, most important step is to kno... thing.
- You take it fi...
- Some people... than others t...
- Everyone wh... passed this c... everything.

The first, most in... to knowing every... remembering eve... everyone has eve...

This doesn't take... Every time you h... thing you haven't... fore, commit it t... This doesn't take...

Tips On Everything

Contrary to popular belief, it is possible to know everything. And the surprising thing is, it takes a lot less time and energy than you might think.

Did you know that it is possible to know everything. And the surprising thing is, it takes a lot less time and energy than you might think.

Light vertical lines separate text columns in a workbook that was formatted to look like a newsletter. Columns do not always need vertical lines between them. If a page with columns looks busy, try increasing the space between columns instead of using lines.

Knowing Everything: Simpler Than You Might Think!

Contrary to popular belief, it *is* possible to know everything. And the surprising thing is, it takes a lot less time and energy than you might think.

The first, most important step to knowing everything is remembering everything that everyone has ever told you. This doesn't take much effort. Every time you hear something you haven't heard before, commit it to memory immediately. Second, it is very important to remember everything you read or see on TV.

"Just when you think you know it all, you meet someone who knows more than you do."

On Being a Know-It-All: Suprisingly Rewarding and Useful!

Contrary to popular belief, it *is* possible to know everything. And the surprising thing is, it takes a lot less time and energy than you might think.

The first, most important step to knowing everything is remembering everything that everyone has ever told you. This doesn't take much effort. Every time you hear something you haven't heard before, commit it to memory immediately.

Second, it is very... see on T.V. An ea... ber is: if it contain... Generally, this m... remember to do th...

Contrary to popu... the surprising thi... might think.

Remembering Everything: The First Step

Contrary to popul... the surprising thi... might think.

The first, most im... bering everything... take much effort.

Every time you h... it to memory imm...

Remembering Everything

Heavy lines emphasize a quote separated from the main text. A quote set off like this is called a "pull quote."

Wanting to Know More

The first step to knowing more is wanting to know more. In order to have the level of dedication required to remember everything your hear, read, or see, you must be completely committed to knowing more.

Knowing more always requires wanting to know more. In order to have the level of dedication required to remember everything your hear, read, or see, you must be completely committed to knowing more. You may want to begin by asking yourself these questions:

- What kind of knowledge do you want?
- Is it possible you only want to know a little more and not everything?
- How do your friends feel about the prospect of you knowing everything?

Keep in mind that the first step to knowing more is wanting to know more. In order to have the level of dedication required to remember everything your hear, read, or see, you must be completely committed to knowing more..

Keep in mind that the first step to knowing more is wanting to know more. In order to have the level of dedication required to remember everything your hear, read, or see, you must be completely committed to knowing more. Don't forget that in order to have the level of dedication required to remember everything your hear, read, or see, you must be completely committed to knowing more..

If you know	Try this ...
Enough to get by, but not everything	• Concentrate on what new things you have yet to learn. • Realize that some is not enough.
A little of everything, but not everything	• Understand how much more clearly you'll see the world once you know more than a little.
Too much to know any more	• Realize that in terms of knowledge, there is no "too much." • Keep concentrating on the advantages to knowing too much.

To improve your knowledge level, concentrate and practice.

2

Intersecting lines draw attention to the title and provide a frame for the text. Horizontal lines separate blocks of information in the table.

Don't put text too close to a line. Space above and below a line makes the words easier to read.

✗ No

RULES OF THUMB

Heading Heading

✔ Yes

RULES OF THUMB

Heading Heading

If you put a line across the top of a page, don't put a heavier line across the bottom. Use a line of equal weight, lighter weight, or no line. The page will look more balanced.

✗ No

✔ Yes

The one point and the half-point line weights used together in the first example do not provide much contrast. By making the difference in line weights more obvious, you gain contrast and a stronger design.

✗ No　　　　　　　　　　　　1 pt.

Write answers below.

1. ＿＿＿＿＿＿＿＿＿＿＿＿＿ .5 pt.
2. ＿＿＿＿＿＿＿＿＿＿＿＿＿
3. ＿＿＿＿＿＿＿＿＿＿＿＿＿
4. ＿＿＿＿＿＿＿＿＿＿＿＿＿

✔ Yes　　　　　　　　　　　　2 pt.

Write answers below.

1. ＿＿＿＿＿＿＿＿＿＿＿＿＿ .5 pt.
2. ＿＿＿＿＿＿＿＿＿＿＿＿＿
3. ＿＿＿＿＿＿＿＿＿＿＿＿＿
4. ＿＿＿＿＿＿＿＿＿＿＿＿＿

Tables do not always need vertical lines. Depending on the content, a table can be just as easy to use, and look cleaner and simpler, without them.

Title of Table			
item	item	item	item
item	item	item	item
item	item	item	item

Title of Table			
item	item	item	item
item	item	item	item
item	item	item	item

4

BOXES

Look at a few pages of training materials, and you're likely to find at least one box, if not half a dozen. Boxes are overused in training materials, especially double- and triple-line boxes around tables.

Boxes do have many useful functions, however. They can be used to:

- Emphasize important information

- Set off subordinate information

- Contain an illustration, chart, or graph

- Define space for writing

- Create a border around a page

As with lines, think about why you are using a box. Do you really need it? Is there another way to treat the information? Not all tables, for example, need to be boxed (see "Tables"on page 54). And there are other ways to emphasize information; for example, by indenting it or making the type larger (see "Creating Emphasis" on page 22).

This chapter shows examples of boxes used effectively.

Examples of boxes

Boxes can be created with a variety of borders. A word processing program offers a few choices; a page layout program offers more. Clip art and graphics programs allow you to create custom borders.

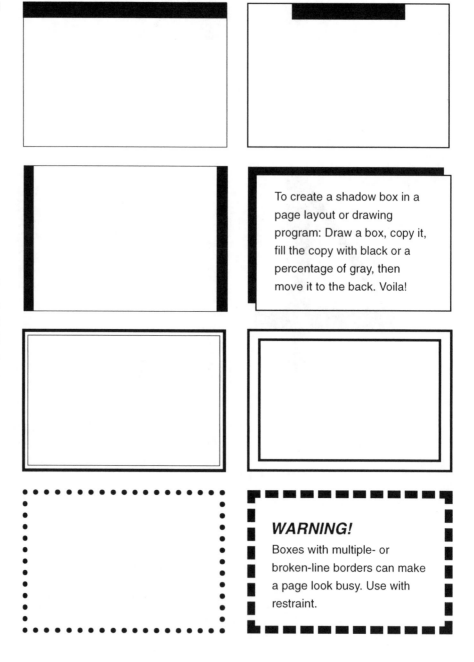

To create a shadow box in a page layout or drawing program: Draw a box, copy it, fill the copy with black or a percentage of gray, then move it to the back. Voila!

WARNING!
Boxes with multiple- or broken-line borders can make a page look busy. Use with restraint.

GUIDELINES for using boxes

- Don't use too many boxes on a page; one large or three small ones is enough.

- Leave space both inside and outside the box.

- Leave more space around a heavy border.

- Don't use busy borders.

You can create many different looks.

1. This text is not in a box. Why not? Because this information has already been set off by putting it in a list and numbering each item.

2. This is an example of a situation in which you might not need a box.

3. The next time you're ready to put a box around something that is already in list form, ask yourself if the box is really necessary.

You can create many different looks by varying the typeface and how you use white space inside a box. You can create many different looks by varying the typeface and how you use white space inside a box. You can create many different looks.

Border, typeface, and white space create the look of the box.

"A box is a box is a box is a box..."

The triangular shadow behind this box was created in a drawing program.

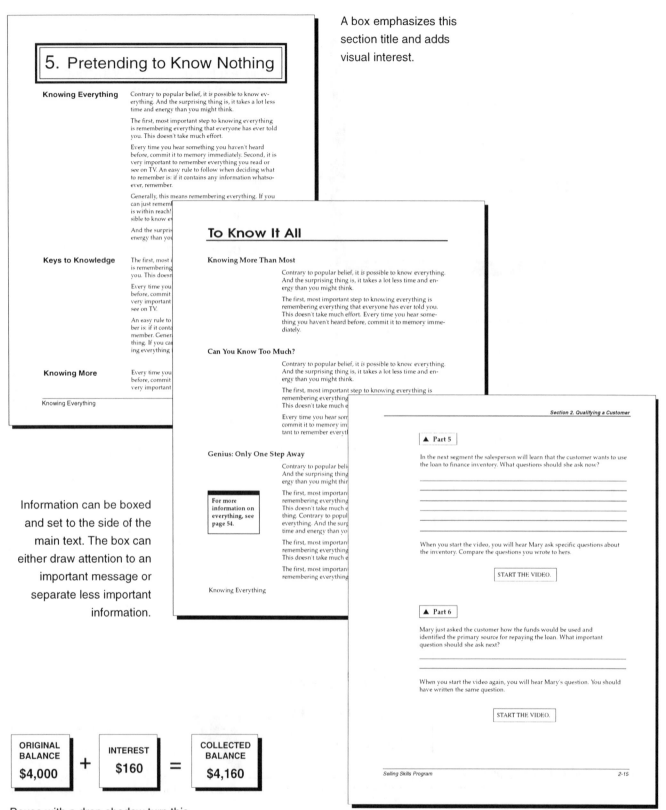

A box emphasizes this section title and adds visual interest.

5. Pretending to Know Nothing

Knowing Everything

Contrary to popular belief, it *is* possible to know everything. And the surprising thing is, it takes a lot less time and energy than you might think.

The first, most important step to knowing everything is remembering everything that everyone has ever told you. This doesn't take much effort.

Every time you hear something you haven't heard before, commit it to memory immediately. Second, it is very important to remember everything you read or see on TV. An easy rule to follow when deciding what to remember is: if it contains any information whatsoever, remember.

Generally, this means remembering everything. If you can just remem... is within reach! sible to know e...

And the surpris... energy than you...

Keys to Knowledge

The first, most i... is remembering... you. This doesn...

Every time you... before, commit... very important... see on TV.

An easy rule to... ber is: if it conta... member. Gener... thing. If you ca... ing everything...

Knowing More

Every time you... before, commit... very important...

Knowing Everything

To Know It All

Knowing More Than Most

Contrary to popular belief, it *is* possible to know everything. And the surprising thing is, it takes a lot less time and energy than you might think.

The first, most important step to knowing everything is remembering everything that everyone has ever told you. This doesn't take much effort. Every time you hear something you haven't heard before, commit it to memory immediately.

Can You Know Too Much?

Contrary to popular belief, it *is* possible to know everything. And the surprising thing is, it takes a lot less time and energy than you might think.

The first, most important step to knowing everything is remembering everything... This doesn't take much e...

Every time you hear som... commit it to memory im... tant to remember everyth...

Genius: Only One Step Away

Contrary to popular beli... And the surprising thing... ergy than you might thin...

The first, most importan... remembering everything... This doesn't take much e... thing. Contrary to popul... everything. And the sur... time and energy than yo...

The first, most importan... remembering everything... This doesn't take much e...

The first, most importan... remembering everything...

> For more information on everything, see page 54.

Knowing Everything

Information can be boxed and set to the side of the main text. The box can either draw attention to an important message or separate less important information.

▲ Part 5

In the next segment the salesperson will learn that the customer wants to use the loan to finance inventory. What questions should she ask now?

_____
_____
_____
_____
_____

When you start the video, you will hear Mary ask specific questions about the inventory. Compare the questions you wrote to hers.

START THE VIDEO.

▲ Part 6

Mary just asked the customer how the funds would be used and identified the primary source for repaying the loan. What important question should she ask next?

_____
_____

When you start the video again, you will hear Mary's question. You should have written the same question.

START THE VIDEO.

| ORIGINAL BALANCE $4,000 | + | INTEREST $160 | = | COLLECTED BALANCE $4,160 |

Boxes with a drop shadow turn this equation into a bold graphic and make it easier to remember.

Boxes set off section numbers and instructions in this interactive workbook.

Knowing It All

1 **Study everything.**

The only way to really know it all is to study everything all the time. It's really not that hard to do. Just pay close attention to everything at all times, take notes, and then study everything until you remember all of it.

2 **Don't forget anything.**

The only way to really know it all is to study everything all the time. It's really not that hard to do. Just pay close attention to everything at all times, take notes, and then study everything until you remember all of it. The only way to really know it all is to study everything all the time.

3 **Pay close attention to everything.**

The only way to really know it all is to study everythi hard to do. Just pay close attention to everything a study everything until you remember all of it. The onl study everything all the time.

4 **Take notes.**

The only way to really know it all is to study everythi hard to do. Just pay close attention to everything a study everything until you remember all of it. The onl study everything all the time.

The only way to really know it all is to study everythi hard to do. Then study everything until you remembe know it all is to study everything all the time.

5 **Concentrate on knowing it all.**

The only way to really know it all is to study everythi hard to do. Just pay close attention to everything a study everything until you remember all of it. The onl study everything all the time.

Knowing It All

A box drawn with a light line creates a simple border around the page.

Review Questions

Write your answers in the boxes provided.

1. What are five ways to remember everything?

2. Watch the video. Which character clearly knows everything?

3. Which character seems to know everything but actually doesn't? Would you want to use this method? Why or why not?

4. What did you learn about knowing ever

Boxes can define space for writing answers to questions.

KNOWLEDGE

Knowing Everything

In order to know everything about every-thing, it is very important that you read everything in this self-study. Knowledge of everything is now within your grasp. All you need to do is read this self-study and answer all of the questions, and you will know everything. In order to know every-thing about everything, it is very important that you read everything in this self-study.

Reading Everything

Knowledge of everything is now within your grasp. All you need to do is read this self-study and answer all of the questions, and you will know everything. In order to know everything about everything there is to know, it is very important that you read absolutely every single thing that is found in this self-study.

Knowledge of everything is now within your grasp. All you need to do is read this self-study and answer all of the questions, and you will know everything. In order to know everything about everything, it is very important that you read everything in this self-study. Knowledge of everything is now within your grasp. All you need to do is read this self-study and answer all of the questions, and you will know everything. In order to know everything about everything, it is very important that you read everything in this self-study. Knowledge of everything is now within your grasp.

Two More Tips

• It is very important that you read everything in this self-study. Knowledge of everything is now within your grasp.

• All you need to do is read this self-study and answer all of the ques-tions, and you will know every-thing. In order to know everything about everything, it is very impor-tant that you read everything in this self-study.

Remembering Everything

All you need to do is read this self-study and answer all of the questions, and you will know everything. In order to know everything about everything, it is very important that you read everything in this self-study.

In order to know everything about everything, it is very important that you read everything in this self-study. Knowledge of everything is now within your grasp. Isn't it great to finally know

Knowledge Workbook   *1*

One box frames the clip art image; the other separates information from the main text. A box set apart from the main text like this is called a "sidebar."

Several boxes are used on this page, but the effect is not overdone. There are two shaded boxes, two boxes with reverse type in them, and a box of bulleted items. Square bullets add to the repetition.

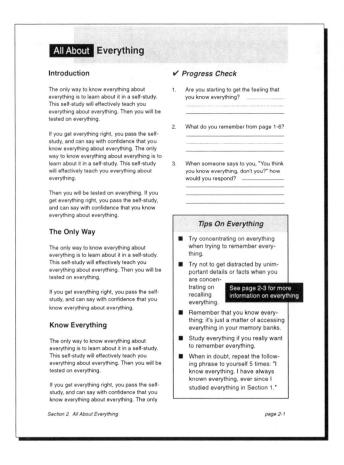

All About Everything

Introduction

The only way to know everything about everything is to learn about it in a self-study. This self-study will effectively teach you everything about everything. Then you will be tested on everything.

If you get everything right, you pass the self-study, and can say with confidence that you know everything about everything. The only way to know everything about everything is to learn about it in a self-study. This self-study will effectively teach you everything about everything.

Then you will be tested on everything. If you get everything right, you pass the self-study, and can say with confidence that you know everything about everything.

The Only Way

The only way to know everything about everything is to learn about it in a self-study. This self-study will effectively teach you everything about everything. Then you will be tested on everything.

If you get everything right, you pass the self-study, and can say with confidence that you know everything about everything.

Know Everything

The only way to know everything about everything is to learn about it in a self-study. This self-study will effectively teach you everything about everything. Then you will be tested on everything.

If you get everything right, you pass the self-study, and can say with confidence that you know everything about everything. The only

✔ *Progress Check*

1. Are you starting to get the feeling that you know everything? _____
   _____
   _____

2. What do you remember from page 1-6?
   _____
   _____
   _____

3. When someone says to you, "You think you know everything, don't you?" how would you respond? _____
   _____
   _____

Tips On Everything

■ Try concentrating on everything when trying to remember everything.

■ Try not to get distracted by unimportant details or facts when you are concentrating on recalling everything.
   See page 2-3 for more information on everything

■ Remember that you know everything; it's just a matter of accessing everything in your memory banks.

■ Study everything if you really want to remember everything.

■ When in doubt, repeat the following phrase to yourself 5 times: "I know everything. I have always known everything, ever since I studied everything in Section 1."

Section 2. All About Everything   *page 2-1*

Rounded corners on a box aren't very interesting. Square corners look stronger and more authoritative.

✗ No

Two Easy Steps

1. Read everything.

2. Remember all of it.

✔ Yes

Two Easy Steps

1. Read everything.

2. Remember all of it.

Don't put text too close to the border of a box. Boxes need space in and around them.

✗ No

cyberspace unmapped online territory

e-mail electronic message system

Ezra online psychologist

Internet thousands of electronic networks

✔ Yes

cyberspace unmapped online territory

e-mail electronic message system

Ezra online psychologist

Internet thousands of electronic networks

5

SHADING

The option called *shading* or *fill* on the menu of your software program is technically called *grayscale* or *screens* in graphic design terminology. Shading is a percentage of black, ranging from 5 percent (light gray) to 100 percent (solid black).

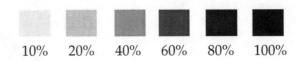

10%   20%   40%   60%   80%   100%

Shading can add color, drama, and elegance to pages printed in black and white.

Whether the result is truly elegant or just gray, however, depends on the process used to print your materials. For example, a corporate training department might download its text files to a printing service that makes a film negative and prints from that, and the shading will be printed at the highest possible resolution. Someone writing user guides for a small software company may not be able to use any shading because the manuals are printed at a local quick-print shop where all the shaded areas turn dark or uneven.

Whatever printing method you use, the final version is likely to look different from the masters produced on your laser printer.

If your materials will be printed on an imagesetter like the Linotronic, you may have to reduce or increase the percentage of shading on your computer to get the result you want. Percentages under 50 percent will print lighter on an imagesetter than they do on a laser printer; percentages over 50 percent will print darker than on a laser printer.

For the best results, talk to your printing service and test a few pages.

GUIDELINES for using shading

- Limit shading to one or two percentages on a page.
- Use increments of 10 percent (5 percent is too subtle).
- Use 20 percent or lighter if you'll print text or an image over it.
- For legibility, use bold sans serif type when printing over shading.
- Don't shade large blocks of type; they're hard to read.

✗ No

To be legible, type printed over shading should contrast sharply with the background. This is too dark.

Training for employees who need to know everything.

✔ Yes

For the best results, use bold sans serif type and light shading.

Training for employees who need to know everything.

Examples of shading

A **shadow box** doesn't have to be solid black; it can be gray, as shown here. Also, you may be able to use **shaded bullets** on a checklist or job aid. Draw small boxes with a shaded fill, or use the bullets in a font like Zapf Dingbats and print them in gray if your software prints gray type.

Checklist
- Analysis
- Design
- Development
- Delivery
- Evaluation

Time In Minutes

Month	2	3	4
Exercise	35	66	77
Reading	15	16	17
TV	87	98	90
Sleep	34	45	43

Shading can be used instead of lines to separate **rows or columns** in a table.

Shaded bars can be used instead of lines.

JOB AID

1 This job aid should help you learn everything you need to know about your job.

2 This job aid should help you learn everything you need to know about your job. This job aid should help.

3 This job aid should help you learn everything you need to know about your job.

4 This job aid should help you learn everything you need to know about your job. This job aid should help you.

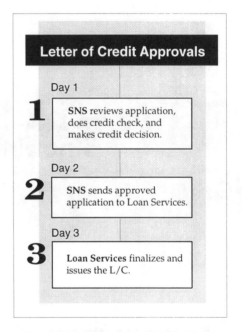

Letter of Credit Approvals

Day 1

1 **SNS** reviews application, does credit check, and makes credit decision.

Day 2

2 **SNS** sends approved application to Loan Services.

Day 3

3 **Loan Services** finalizes and issues the L/C.

A **shaded background** adds depth and makes these boxes stand out.

Type can be printed in the color gray in some software programs. Use this for a special effect in a title or on a cover page. Make **gray type** large or it will not be legible.

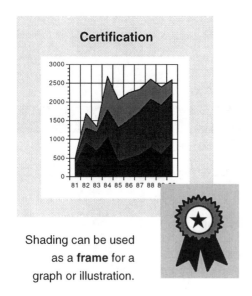

Certification

Shading can be used
as a **frame** for a
graph or illustration.

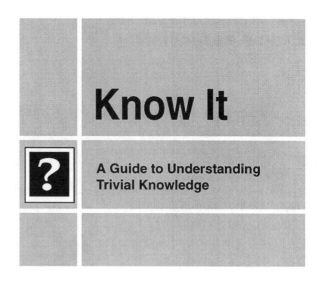

Know It

? **A Guide to Understanding
Trivial Knowledge**

White lines on a shaded background can dress up a
title page.

**Answers to
Progress Check**

1 $10

2 $3

3 567

4 700

Fill the holes in your knowledge and start
Knowing Everything

White images can be "popped out" of a
shaded background.

Shading can **highlight fields** on an
example of a computer screen.

```
ARCN   REVENUE ASSESSMENT FORM CORRECTIONS  DATE   PAGE 01
WB: 687 889864 8125
ERROR:   AUTH   CRT: 3492993990


ADVANCE      PRE-PAID        RATE           DESC         PACKAGE
--           5556768         00000 00       002145       3343
--           5556769         00000 00       INV898       3344
```

Callouts can be put in a shaded box,
with or without a line border.

**If description number is
invalid, type INV in the
DESC field.**

A grayscale image, such as a simple logo or this map of the world, can be used as a **background**. Make sure the image is not busy and that anything printed over it stands out sharply.

A **gradient** grayscale (also called a *blend* or *graduated fill*) can create a subtle color change. Not all software provides this option.

Knowledge of Everything
Self-Study

This grayscale **shadow image**, created to look like torn paper, was drawn in a graphics program.

Knowing Everything
The Ultimate Resource Guide

Using more than two percentages of shading together is risky for the non-designer. This graphic for a workbook title page uses four percentages, plus black type. It's a good design, but a high-quality printing process is necessary for the best results. The "4" is in Neuland, a typeface useful only for decorative purposes.

ABCDEF1234567890
Neuland

This version uses only two percentages of shading, plus black and white type. Unless you really trust your graphic design skills and your printing process is high quality, limit shading to one or two percentages.

6 GRAPHICS

Graphics are everywhere — in newspapers and magazines, on TV weather reports, on CD-ROM encyclopedias. They play an increasingly important role in communicating information, and in printed training materials.

Graphics include not just illustrations such as clip art and drawings of equipment, but also tables, charts, and graphs. Even when tables and charts consist mostly of words, they provide a visual break from paragraphs of text.

Effectively used, graphics attract attention, make materials more interesting, reduce the need for so many words, and make information easier to find, understand, and remember. These claims are supported by research.

If you haven't been using graphics in your materials, experiment with including them. For example:

- Use a diagram to illustrate a process.

- Combine visuals and words to explain a complex subject.

- Use a visual analogy to make an abstract concept more concrete.

- Create a cartoon character to convey an important message.

Learning to think visually is a skill that can be developed, and there are references in the Appendixes to help you.

Although the purpose of graphics is primarily to communicate, even graphics for decoration have a place in training materials. For example, a small visual can break up long passages of text; a company or product logo can provide a visual motif.

If your audience is diverse or likely to include visual learners (who prefer graphics), graphics are especially important. Many training materials could benefit from a complete "re-engineering" to incorporate more graphics.

This chapter is full of ideas and guidelines to help you use graphics effectively.

GUIDELINES for using graphics

- Use graphics that are appropriate for your subject and audience.

- Keep the style consistent throughout a document or series of graphics.

- Keep graphics simple.

- Make graphics pleasing to look at.

- Before you buy a clip art package, do research and ask questions:

    - Are the images appropriate for your audience? Consider age, ethnicity, sex, and other characteristics.

    - Will the images help you communicate your ideas?

    - Will the file format of the clip art work with your software?

    - What will the images look like printed on your printer? This could be quite different from the way they look in the catalog.

- Don't use scanned, traced, or photocopied images that are copyrighted. Clip art is copyright-free, but many other images are not.

Icons and symbols

Icons and symbols should be **simple**. Keep unnecessary details out of the image.

Use symbols that are immediately **recognizable and familiar** to readers. Note: The hand symbol here is familiar to American audiences, but it may have an entirely different meaning elsewhere in the world.

Make each icon or symbol **visually distinct**. Even though these two symbols from a leader's guide are labeled, an instructor will recognize them more quickly when they look distinctly different.

Maintain a **consistent** visual style throughout a document.

All these symbols are crisp and bold.

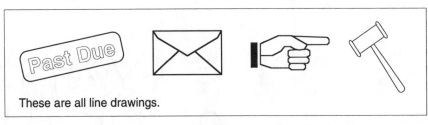

These are all line drawings.

Always test icons and symbols on users. Also, try printing an icon or symbol in the smallest size it will appear in your materials to make sure it is legible.

People

Clip art people range in style from silhouettes to detailed drawings to whimsical characters. Be sure to use a style that suits your subject and audience.

PERSUASION   ZEDCOR   T/MAKER CLICKART

If you have a little skill or an artist's services, you can draw your own people. Hiring an artist to create a few custom images may be the best solution when you can't find suitable clip art people.

These were created with shapes and heavy lines. In most cases, it's not necessary to show facial features or details that indicate race or gender.

These were created in a drawing program.

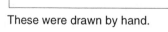
These were drawn by hand.   LYNN KEARNY

Cartoons

Cartoons are useful as long as they are appropriate for your audience and purpose.

They can help you motivate . . .

reinforce a point in a lesson . . .

CREATED IN FREEHAND

lighten up a serious message . . .

or simply add humor.

Flow charts and diagrams

Be sure to keep flow charts simple. Shading and reverse type can enhance a flow chart by adding contrast.

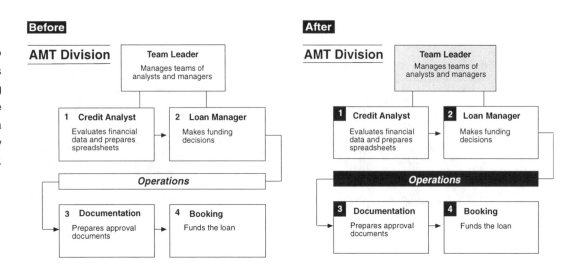

Use arrows or clear symbols to indicate direction. Limit the number of symbols to five or six per diagram. If a chart or diagram is too large, try subdividing it and showing the parts separately.

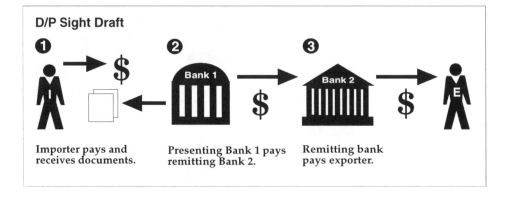

Don't show more detail or background in a diagram than is necessary. A simple line drawing is usually the most effective. It focuses attention on what's important and makes the image easier to remember.

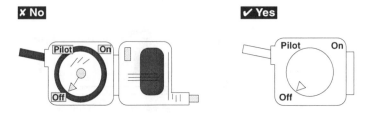

Graphs and charts

Readers should be able to understand graphs at a glance. Keep them as simple as possible. Put the details about the graph in the text of the learning materials, not on the graph itself.

To show	Use this chart/graph
Trends	Line
Comparison of values	Bar/column; pictograph
Proportions of the whole	Pie

GUIDELINES for any kind of graph

- Avoid vertical text labels.
- When possible, put labels on the graph itself so a legend or grid becomes unnecessary. But don't clutter the graph.
- If you use a grid, use very fine lines or white lines on a shaded background, and use as few lines as possible.
- Don't use less than four or more than ten steps in the scale on the X and Y axes.
- Use upper- and lower-case type for labels, 8 points minimum.
- A box around the graph is often unnecessary.

Line graphs

- Show no more than four or five lines.
- The boldest line should be the one you want to emphasize.

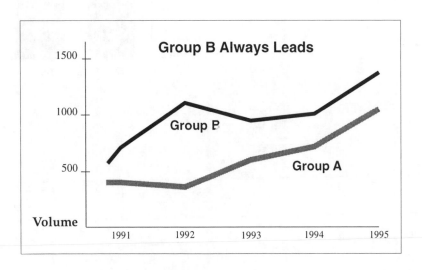

Bar and column charts

- Avoid multiple shadings, patterns, drop shadows, and special effects because they distract learners. (Some software programs automatically create such effects; do the best you can within their limits.)

- Minimize the use of grid lines and vertical text labels. See the guidelines for all graphs on page 51.

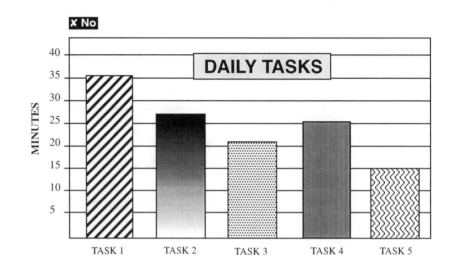

- Make bars and columns wider than the spaces between them. The space should not be less than 25% of the bar or column width.

- The tallest column or longest bar should be at least 75% of the height or width of the graph.

- If the bars or columns are shaded, there is no need to outline them as well.

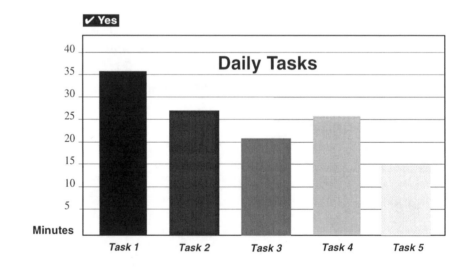

Pie charts

- Avoid tiny segments because they're too hard to read.
- Put the edge of the largest segment at the 12 o'clock position because people read clockwise.
- Don't make pie charts look three dimensional because it distorts the size of the pieces.

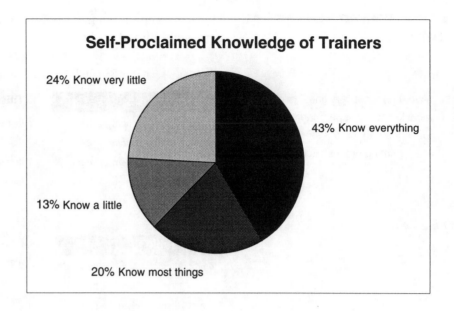

Pictographs

- Use simple, appropriate icons.
- Make all the icons the same size.
- Don't change the size of the icons to represent changes in the data.

Tables

Here are some formats to help you create tables that are not completely lined and boxed-in.

Avoid unnecessary lines, especially vertical lines. Try separating items with space instead, or use shading if your printing process is high quality.

Title of Table			
Item	Item	Item	Item
Item	Item	Item	Item
Item	Item	Item	Item
Item	Item	Item	Item

Title of Table			
Item	Item	Item	Item
Item	Item	Item	Item
Item	Item	Item	Item
Item	Item	Item	Item

Title of Table			
Item	Item	Item	Item
Item	Item	Item	Item
Item	Item	Item	Item
Item	Item	Item	Item

Title of Table			
Item	Item	Item	Item
Item	Item	Item	Item
Item	Item	Item	Item
Item	Item	Item	Item

Use thin lines when you do use lines.

Title of Table			
Item	Item	Item	Item
Item	Item	Item	Item
Item	Item	Item	Item
Item	Item	Item	Item

Title of Table			
Item	Item	Item	Item
Item	Item	Item	Item
Item	Item	Item	Item
Item	Item	Item	Item

Put column and row headings in bold, italics, shading, or a contrasting typeface to make them stand out.

Title of Table			
Item	**Item**	**Item**	**Item**
Item	Item	Item	Item
Item	Item	Item	Item
Item	Item	Item	Item

Title of Table			
Item	Item	Item	Item
Item	Item	Item	Item
Item	Item	Item	Item
Item	Item	Item	Item

It's okay to make a table wider than the text blocks on a page if necessary.

Label				Label
	item	item	item	
	item	item	item	
	item	item	item	

Avoid vertical text labels because they're hard to read. (Avoid them anywhere, not just in tables.)

Proportion and placement

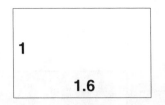
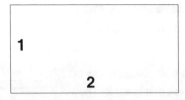

Two of the most aesthetically pleasing shapes for a graphic are rectangles of these proportions.

If a graphic is framed, a wider margin at the bottom will make it look more balanced.

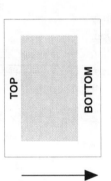

On a page that must be turned sideways to be viewed, put the bottom of the graphic to the right. Do this for a right- or left-hand page.

Place graphics where they are first referred to in the text, even if doing so creates extra blank space at the bottom of the page. Repeat the graphic if necessary (maybe in a smaller size, or by showing only relevant parts) rather than require learners to keep turning back to it.

GUIDELINES for size

- Make graphics **larger** if:
    - they are intended to motivate or get attention
    - they will be viewed in low light
    - readers have only a short time to look at them
    - readers are vision-impaired
- Show computer screens at 50 to 75 percent of actual size; this is usually adequate.
- In general, graphics can be **smaller** than you would expect and still be effective.

Captions and titles

Captions are best placed below or to the side of a graphic. They should be aligned with one edge of the graphic or centered along the side. Use left or right aligned text, as indicated in this illustration.

Distinguish captions from body text by using smaller type, boldface, italics, or a contrasting typeface.

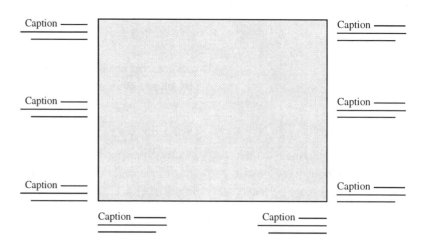

Put each caption with the graphic it describes, not on a separate page or a different part of the page where it may be confused with the surrounding text.

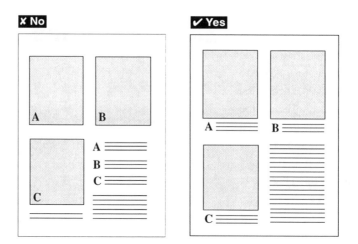

Put the title above a graphic (unless it is part of the caption).

Centering the title over a graphic can help to differentiate it from the text that precedes it. However, graphic designers strongly prefer left justified titles. If a title is over three lines, left justify it.

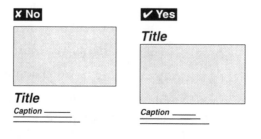

Labels and callout lines

Put labels on or close to the graphic so it is immediately clear what a label refers to.

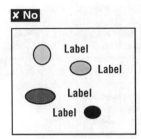

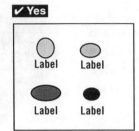

Don't clutter a graphic with lines or labels.

A small dot or arrow at the end of a callout line can focus attention and help identify what the line points to.

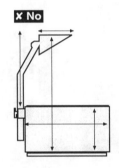

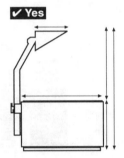

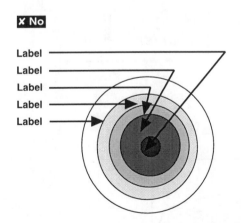

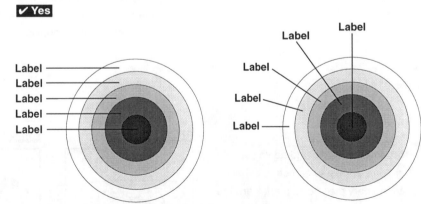

This graphic looks better without arrows, and with parallel or diagonal callout lines. Both revisions take up less space than the original. If you use callout lines, use short, light lines. If possible, align the edges of labels.

Special effects

A **decorative graphic** like this can add visual interest. This was created in a page layout program by placing white text over a rotated black square.

Create a picture by **combining and resizing clip art.** Here the standing man and woman are repeated in smaller sizes to form a line of people.

Extending an illustration outside the border of a box is a graphic design trick to add visual interest.

Go to
Chapter 7

Rotating an image and adding simple graphic elements can often enhance an ordinary piece of clip art. Here the phone was rotated and lines drawn above it to make the phone look like it is ringing.

Before

After

A clip art image can sometimes be **compacted or stretched**. This city skyline looks good in all three versions, but not all images will look good distorted.

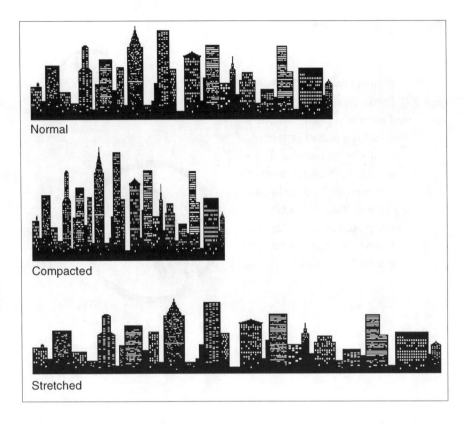

Normal

Compacted

Stretched

When **wrapping text** around a graphic, don't leave a wide gap of white space. Wrap the text close to the graphic, within the limits of your software program. This is easier to achieve in a page layout program than a word processing program.

✘ No

Lorem ipsum dolor sit amet, consectetuer adipiscing elit, sed diam nonummy nibh euismod tincidunt ut laoreet dolore magna aliquam erat volutpat. Ut wisi enim ad minim veniam, quis nos trud exerci tation ullam corper suscipit lobortis nisl ut aliquip ex e a commodo consequat. Lorem ipsum dolor sit amet, consectetuer adipiscing elit, sed diam nonummy nibh euismod tincidunt ut laoreet dolore magna aliquam erat volutpat. Ut wisi enim ad minim veniam, quis nostrud exerci tation ullamcorper suscipit lobortis nisl

✔ Yes

Lorem ipsum dolor sit amet, consectetuer adipiscing elit, sed diam nonummy nibh euismod tincidunt ut laoreet dolore magna aliquam erat volutpat. Ut wisi enim ad minim veniam, quis nos trud exerci tation ullam corper suscipit lobortis nisl ut aliquip ex e a commodo consequat. Lorem ipsum dolor sit amet, consectetuer adipiscing elit, sed diam nonummy nibh euismod tincidunt ut laoreet dolore magna aliquam erat volutpat. Ut wisi enim ad minim veniam, quis nostrud exerci tation ullamcorper suscipit lobortis nisl ut aliquip ex ea commodo. consequat. Lorem ipsum dolor sit amet, consectetuer adipiscing elit, sed diam nonummy nibh euismod tincidunt ut laoreet dolore magna aliquam erat

Playing with fonts

Symbol or picture fonts are a simple way to add graphics to your materials. Each character in the font is a picture instead of a letter of the alphabet. These images don't take up as much disk space as other kinds of graphics. You can print them in any point size. Zapf Dingbats, shown here, is one of the most common. There are many more.

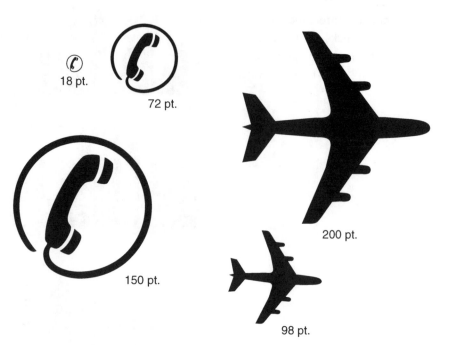

18 pt.

72 pt.

150 pt.

200 pt.

98 pt.

The Adobe Cheq font is designed specifically to create a chess board. It is used here to create a graphic for the title of a workbook. Though this may look complex to create, it isn't with this font. (The dollar sign is a different font.)

A big ampersand in certain fonts can be dramatic.

Bookman Bold 100 pt.

Times Bold 150 pt.

Page number graphics

Turning the page number into a graphic can enhance a workbook, job aid, or set of handouts, and provide a repeated graphic. Here are some ideas.

Note: Most of these can be created only in a page layout program.

Numbers in lists

Training materials often present information in numbered steps. Here are some formats you might use to dress up the numbers.

Note: Most of these can be created only in a page layout program.

3 Lorem ipsum dolor sit amet, consectetuer adipiscing elit, sed diam nonummy nibh euismod tincidunt ut

3 Lorem ipsum sit amet, consect adipiscing elit, sed diam non ummy nibh euismod tincidunt ut

③ Lorem ipsum dolor sit amet, consectetuer adipiscing elit, sed diam non ummy nibh euismod tincidunt ut

3 Lorem ipsum dolor sit amet, consec tetuer adipiscing elit, sed diam nonummy nibh

3 Lorem ipsum dolor sit amet, consectetuer adipiscing elit, sed diam nonummy nibh euismod tincidunt ut

3 Lorem ipsum dolor sit amet, consectetuer adipiscing elit, sed diam nonummy nibh euismod tincidunt ut

3 Lorem ipsum dolor sit amet, consectetuer adipiscing elit, sed diam nonummy nibh euismod tincidunt ut laoreet dolore

3 Lorem ipsum dolor sit amet, consec tetuer adipiscing elit, sed diam nonummy nibh euismod tincidunt ut

3 Lorem ipsum dolor sit amet, consectetuer adipiscing elit, sed diam nonummy nibh euismod tincidunt ut

③ Lorem ipsum dolor sit amet, consectetuer adipiscing elit, sed diam nonummy nibh

3 Lorem ipsum dolor sit amet, consectetuer adipiscing elit, sed diam nonummy nibh euismod

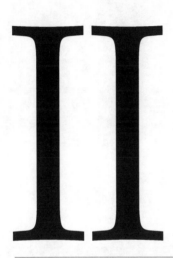

Examples of Training Materials

7
WORKBOOKS

People use workbooks in a class or on their own to complete a self-paced course. Workbooks usually include exercises and quizzes or tests, with space to work out problems and write answers.

When employees open a workbook, they should see something that piques their interest or makes them feel the learning task might be enjoyable. They should not find a gray mass of text that looks overwhelming or intimidating. Although some subjects are by nature more tedious than others, and some do require multiple pages of explanation, good graphic design can make any workbook pleasing to look at and inviting to use.

Most workbooks are created in one of the three basic formats shown on page 67. Two workbooks in the same format can look very different from one another, depending on how you use type, lines, boxes, shading, and graphics in designing each one.

This chapter shows an example of each format, plus a few workbook covers.

Workbook covers

Employee Training Series
Customer Service Skills Workshop

■ Introduction   1
■ Basic Skills   9
■ Practice   21
■ Difficult Situations 27
■ Practice   40
■ Tips   52

Title
Helvetica Bold 36 pt.
Contents
Helvetica Bold 14 pt.
Footer
Helvetica 12 pt. ▼

Crane-Simpson
International

Performance Planning and Appraisal

Module 2

© Crane-Simpson International, Inc.
May 1995

▲
Large title
Helvetica Bold 48 pt.
Series title
Helvetica Bold 24 pt.
Contents
Helvetica Bold 18 pt.

Employee Workbook

1. Introduction
2. Customer Service
3. Management
4. Internal Communications
5. Meeting Challenges
6. Long-term Vision
7. Policy Changes

© 1995 Martin Lewis Inc.

▲
Title
Bookman Bold 42 pt.
Logo
Created in PageMaker
All other type
Bookman 14 pt.

Three basic formats

Format 1

Headings are on the left-hand side of the page, text is on the right. Examples are on pages 68 and 78.

Here are three frequently used formats for workbooks. Each can present information in a visually interesting way, depending on how you design it.

Format 1 sample page

Heading Heading

Lorem ipsum dolor sit amet, consectetuer adipiscing elit, sed diam nonummy nibh euismod tincidunt ut laoreet dolore magna aliquam erat volutpat. Ut wisi enim ad minim veniam, quis nostrud exerci tation ullamcorper suscipit lobortis nisl ut aliquip ex ea commodo consequat.

Duis autem vel eum iriure dolor in hendrerit in vulputate velit esse molestie consequat, vel illum dolore eu feugiat nulla facilisis at vero eros et accumsan et iusto odio dignissim qui blandit praesent luptatum zzril delenit augue duis dolore te feugait nulla facilisi. Lorem ipsum dolor sit amet, consectetuer adipiscing elit, sed diam nonummy nibh euismod tincidunt ut laoreet dolore magna aliquam erat volutpat.

Subheading Subheading Ut wisi enim ad minim veniam, quis nostrud exerci tation ullamcorper suscipit lobortis nisl ut aliquip ex ea commodo consequat.

Duis autem vel eum iriure dolor in hendrerit in vulputate velit esse molestie consequat eros et accumsan luptatum zzril del

Heading Heading Heading Nam liber tempor imperdiet doming Lorem ipsum dol nonummy nibh eu erat volutpat. Ut tation ullamcorpe consequat.

Duis autem vel eu molestie consequa eros et accumsan luptatum zzril del Lorem ipsum dol nonummy nibh eu erat volutpat.

Ut wisi enim ad m

Footer: Title of Document

Headings stretch across the page and are not confined to the left-hand column. Text may be indented under the headings, as shown here, or aligned with the headings. An example is on page 70.

Format 2

Format 2 sample page

Heading Heading

Lorem ipsum dolor sit amet, consectetuer adipiscing elit, sed diam nonummy nibh euismod tincidunt ut laoreet dolore magna aliquam erat volutpat. Ut wisi enim ad minim veniam, quis nostrud exerci tation ullamcorper suscipit lobortis nisl ut aliquip ex ea commodo consequat. Duis autem vel eum iriure dolor in hendrerit in vulputate.

Lorem ipsum dolor sit amet, consectetuer adipiscing elit, sed diam nonummy nibh euismod tincidunt ut laoreet dolore magna aliquam erat volutpat. Ut wisi enim ad minim veniam, quis nostrud exerci tation ullamcorper suscipit lobortis nisl ut aliquip ex ea commodo consequat. Duis autem vel eum iriure dolor in hendrerit in vulputate velit esse molestie consequat, vel illum dolore eu feugiat nulla facilisis at vero eros et accumsan et iusto odio dignissim qui blandit praesent luptatum zzril delenit augue duis dolore te feugait nulla facilisi.

Heading Heading Heading

Nam liber tempor cum soluta nobis eleifend option congue nihil imperdiet doming id quod mazim placerat facer possim assum.

- Nam liber tempor cum soluta nobis eleifend quod mazim placerat facer possim a.ssum.
- Ut wisi enim ad minim veniam, quis nostrud
- Ut wisi enim ad minim veniam, quis nostrud lobortis nisl ut aliquip ex ea commodo conse

Subheading

Ut wisi enim ad minim veniam, quis nostrud exerci ta aliquip ex ea commodo consequat. Duis autem vel eu velit esse molestie consequat, vel illum dolore eu feu accumsan et iusto odio dignissim qui blandit praesen te feugait nulla facilisi.

Duis autem vel eum iriure dolor in hendrerit in vulpu illum dolore eu feugiat nulla facilisis at vero eros et a blandit praesent luptatum zzril delenit augue duis dol

- Nam liber tempor cum soluta nobis eleifend quod mazim placerat facer possim assum.

Footer: Title of Document

Text is placed in two columns of equal width. Text is not indented under the headings. An example is on page 74.

Format 3

Format 3 sample page

Heading Heading

Lorem ipsum dolor sit amet, consectetuer adipiscing elit, sed diam nonummy nibh euismod tincidunt ut laoreet dolore magna aliquam erat volutpat. Ut wisi enim ad minim veniam, quis nostrud exerci tation ullamcorper suscipit lobortis nisl ut aliquip ex ea commodo consequat.

Duis autem vel eum iriure dolor in hendrerit in vulputate velit esse molestie consequat, vel illum dolore eu feugiat nulla facilisis at vero eros et accumsan et iusto odio dignissim qui blandit praesent luptatum zzril delenit augue duis dolore te feugait nulla facilisi. Lorem ipsum dolor sit amet, consectetuer adipiscing elit, sed diam nonummy nibh euismod tincidunt ut laoreet dolore magna aliquam erat

Heading Heading

Ut wisi enim ad minim veniam, quis nostrud exerci tation ullamcorper suscipit lobortis nisl ut aliquip ex ea commodo consequat.

Duis autem vel eum iriure dolor in hendrerit in vulputate velit esse molestie consequat, vel illum dolore eu feugiat nulla facilisis at vero eros et accumsan et iusto odio dignissim qui blandit praesent luptatum zzril delenit augue duis dolore te feugait nulla facilisi.

Subheading

Nam liber tempor cum soluta nobis eleifend option congue nihil imperdiet doming id quod mazim placerat facer possim assum. Lorem ipsum dolor sit amet, consectetuer adipiscing elit, sed diam nonummy nibh euismod tincidunt ut laoreet dolore magna aliquam erat volutpat. Ut wisi enim ad minim veniam, quis nostrud exerci tation ullamcorper suscipit lobortis nisl ut aliquip ex ea commodo consequat.

Subheading

Duis autem vel eum iriure dolor in hendrerit in vulputate velit esse molestie consequat, vel illum dolore eu feugiat nulla facilisis at vero eros et accumsan et iusto odio dignissim qui blandit praesent luptatum zzril delenit augue duis dolore te feugait nulla facilisi. Lorem ipsum dolor sit amet, consectetuer adipiscing elit, sed diam nonummy nibh euismod tincidunt ut laoreet dolore magna aliquam erat

Heading Heading

Lorem ipsum dolor sit amet, consectetuer adipiscing elit, sed diam nonummy nibh euismod tincidunt ut laoreet dolore magna aliquam erat volutpat. Ut wisi enim ad minim veniam, quis nostrud exerci tation ullamcorper suscipit lobortis nisl ut aliquip ex ea commodo consequat.

Duis autem vel eum iriure dolor in hendrerit in vulputate velit esse molestie consequat, vel illum dolore eu feugiat nulla facilisis at vero eros et accumsan et iusto odio dignissim qui blandit praesent luptatum zzril delenit augue duis dolore te feugait nulla facilisi. Lorem ipsum dolor sit amet, consectetuer adipiscing elit, sed diam nonummy nibh euismod tincidunt ut laoreet dolore magna aliquam erat volutpat.

Subheading

Nam liber tempor cum soluta nobis eleifend option congue nihil imperdiet doming id quod mazim placerat facer possim assum. Lorem ipsum dolor sit amet, consectetuer adipiscing elit, sed diam nonummy nibh euismod tincidunt ut laoreet dolore magna aliquam erat volutpat.

Ut wisi enim ad minim veniam, quis nostrud exerci tation ullamcorper suscipit lobortis nisl ut aliquip ex ea commodo consequat.

Footer: Title of Document

2

Example 1

These two pages are from a workbook teaching a maintenance crew how to handle breaks in a community water supply. The workbook is used in classroom training and as a field manual. This is an example of basic format 1.

Water Main Breaks

Overview

Water main breaks occur because of natural disasters, earth movement, contractor activities, and material failures. When a break occurs, most of the water released will enter the storm system before a crew arrives. Practices in the section apply to activities **after the flow has been controlled**, for example, pumping out the trench after the main has been repaired.

Major Areas of Responsibility

When controlling a main break, you and your crew will perform the following major tasks as needed:

• Notify District personnel as required (See "Notifying Regulatory Agencies" in this manual.)

• Build filter dams to control sediment.

• Build curb inlet dams to control sediment.

• Build sediment traps.

• Control erosion along the flow path.

• Control pollutants.

• Monitor the discharge water quality.

• Clean up.

Staffing

Distribution Maintenance crew.

Equipment

Main break response truck equipped with:
- sand bags
- tarps
- stakes
- sweeping/cleaning equipment
- chlorine test equipment
- granular activated carbon filter bags
- filter fences
- one inch gravel bags

Water Main Discharges FMP Manual-1994   Page 49

Using short blocks of text, lots of lists, and many graphics is especially important in this workbook because readability is a concern with this audience.

Lots of white space makes the material look easy to understand.

Lightweight lines separate blocks of information.

Use of a bold sans serif typeface for the section title adds contrast to the page.

Notice that the section title is on the right. This makes it easy for users to find when they are flipping through the book.

PROCEDURES

I. **Build Filter Dams
    to Control Sediment**

1. Inspect the discharge and flow path for sediment.

2. If the discharge to the storm drain contains sediments, build gravel or GAC filter bag dams. (This also treats for chlorine, oil, and grease.)

3. Build the dams upstream of the receiving storm drain.

4. Build the dams no greater than curb height and wide enough to minimize flooding.

    See illustration below.

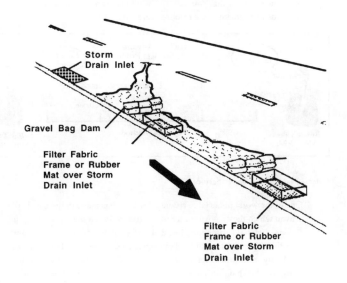

Software
Microsoft Word

Graphics
Drawings scanned into document

Title
Helvetica Bold 18 pt.

Text
Palatino 12 pt.

Headings
Palatino Bold 12 pt.

Footer
Helvetica 10 pt.

Labels on graphic
Helvetica Bold 10 pt.

Example 2

These three pages are from a self-paced workbook used in a sales training program. Learners are college graduates with good reading skills. This is an example of basic format 2.

2 Understanding the Needs of Your Customers

Introduction

Whether your customers are already involved in international trade or are only considering it, their experience in the global market will be very different from their experience doing business domestically. The more you understand about their special conce[...] international trade, the more valuab[...] more receptive they will be to the IT[...] offer. The purpose of this section is t[...] customer's perspective on internatio[...]

By the time you have completed this[...]

- Why companies get involved[...]
- What barriers and risks they f[...]
- Specific concerns of the expor[...]
- How the sales contract addres[...]
- The role of banks and other p[...]

International Trade in California

International trade is vital to Califor[...] country in international trade, handl[...] U.S. imports. California's export vol[...] close to one-fifth of total U.S. export[...] abroad are growing at a rate almost[...] exports are a thriving market in Cali[...]

The illustration below shows the relative risk of the payment methods we've been discussing. You may also want to look at the summary of methods of payment in the resource guide, item 1.1.3.

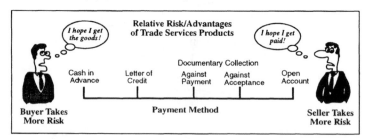

Offering Foreign Exchange Services

One of the worst financial decisions Aloe Care has made in the past is the way in which they have used foreign currency. When they have dealt in dollars, they have sometimes lost their price advantage in a country, and thus their sales, because of foreign currency fluctuations. When they have used only spot contracts, they have not been able to predict their profit margins. They have also felt the effects of foreign currency fluctuation because they have overseas offices that they sent funds to or transferred funds from.

Financing a Company's Trade Cycle

As their relationship manager, you should be aware that not only does a customer's use of Trade Services products indicate a potential foreign exchange exposure, but that all flows of business overseas indicate a potential foreign exchange need. Aloe Care's foreign exchange needs include their L/Cs, D/Ps, D/As, open account terms, and their need to transfer funds to and from their overseas offices.

for any of The Barrel Company's outstanding contracts. Because FX advisors are experts in the foreign currency market, it is best to refer all companies with complex needs to an FX advisor. After you determine their financing needs, The Barrel Company should discuss their options with an FX advisor.

The delivery limit is the maximum that can be settled at one time and is calculated as having 100% risk. The Barrel Company's maximum foreign exchange needs at any one time are $85,000. This is the maximum amount that might be settled at any one time. However, you should set a delivery limit of $200,000, because the delivery limit and the contract limit have a 1:5 relationship. Assuming The Barrel Company qualifies for a credit line of $200,000, you should set a $200,000 delivery limit and a $1 million contract limit.

Here is the proposed facility for The Barrel Company that was calculated in Section 3, with the FX line filled in.

Need	Recommended Facility
L/C Facility	$ 150,000
Financing Need	$ 600,000
FX Line	$200,000
TOTAL (including FX line)	$950,000

Exporter: Aloe Care

 Aloe Care has purchase orders (open account, D/P, D/A, and L/C) for $9,100,000. They have two overseas sales offices (one in Australia and one in Brazil), but no overseas subsidiaries. They are interested in transferring funds to and from their overseas offices. In this case you need to look at the amount they'll need for total sales ($9,100,000), the amount they'll need to move funds to and from their foreign sales offices ($550,000), and any other international flow of business they may be anticipating ($350,000).

This workbook has 12 chapters with lots of narrative. To make the materials visually interesting, every chapter includes one or more cartoons, tables, icons, flow charts, or shaded sidebars.

The large chapter number in reverse type adds a bold graphic to each title page, effectively combining contrast and repetition.

Wide margins and one and one-half line spacing within paragraphs give the pages an open, uncrowded look that compensates for the volume of text.

A cartoon from this workbook is shown on page 49. Cartoons make this potentially tedious subject more interesting, and each one reinforces an important point made in the text.

Software
Microsoft Word
Graphics
Created in FreeHand
Chapter title
Palatino Bold 96 pt.
number and 24 pt. text; created in
Word's graphics window

Text
Palatino 12 pt.
Headings
Level 1: Palatino Bold 13 pt.
Level 2: Palatino Bold Italic 12 pt.
Footer
Palatino 10 pt.

Example 3

These two pages are from a workbook used to train hairstylists in the classroom and on the job. Students are visual learners with little patience for reading dense text. This workbook combines features from basic formats 1 and 2.

Supercuts Tools and Equipment

ACCESSORIES

NECK STRIP

Disposable paper strip that protects the customer's neck from the shampoo cape. Used on every customer with all services.

SUPERCUTS CAPE

Prevents the hair from falling into the customers clothing. The cape is also used to protect the customers clothing from water and products.

WATERBOTTLE

Used to dampen the hair as necessary.

Page 38
© *Copyright 1994 Supercuts*

Use of large, bold type, simple graphics, and plenty of white space makes these pages attractive and inviting to this audience.

The title is placed low on the page, leaving extra white space at the top.

Graphics are simple, bold, and consistent in style; placing them in the same position on each page creates repetition.

Notice the use of proximity — there is more space above headings than below, so each block of text with its heading forms a visual unit, helping learners understand the information more quickly.

These pages show how a heavy, black sans serif typeface can add contrast and drama. The workbook shown on pages 74 and 75 also uses a similar typeface, but the effect is more dramatic here because the type is larger and surrounded by more white space.

Supercuts Tools and Equipment (cont.)

BRUSHES - STYLING & FINISHING

DENMAN BRUSH

Strong, sturdy brush with a soft base of flexible rubber. Rubber brushes do not heat up readily, so they cause less damage to the hair. Excellent for straightening curly hair.

PADDLE BRUSH

Large flat cushion brush used to dry large surfaces efficiently, i.e. long hair.

ROUND BRUSH

Used as a finishing tool for bending any type of hair and can also be used to rearrange waves on curly hair.

SCULPTING BRUSH (Paul Mitchell)

Rubber-cushion based with nylon bristles. The rubber base allows for softer brushing on the hair and scalp. Creates softer movement to the hair for finishing.

VENT BRUSH

Plastic bristle brush with air holes at the base that allows heat to travel through the hair.

Study the definitions of the different brushes.

Then, complete the game on the next page.

Page 39

Software
QuarkXPress

Graphics
Created in
CorelDRAW!

Chapter title
Formata Bold 30 pt.

Text in paragraphs
Caslon and Caslon
Italic 14 pt.

Level 1 headings
Caslon Bold Italic
18 pt.

Level 2 headings
Formata Bold 18 pt.

Header
Formata Bold Italic
12 pt. and
Caslon Italic 12 pt.

Footer
Page numbers
Caslon 10 pt.;
copyright
Caslon Italic 8 pt.

Example 4

These two pages are from a self-paced workbook that teaches financial services employees the basics of their job. The audience is primarily college students with good reading skills. This is an example of basic format 3.

Answers to Check

1. Yes. The ID is not altered and the pictures and signatures match the person standing in front of you. You should write the issuing agency, the number, and the expiration date on the face of the check.

2. Yes. The card she presented uses a traceable number from another institution. You should write her Social Security Number.

3. No. Neither ID contains a picture or physical description of Mrs. Harman. You should ask her for another piece of ID that contains this information. An example of what you might say is, "Mrs. Harman, do you have a piece of ID with your picture on it?"

4. Yes. Since Mr. Hardin is known to you, you can cash his check. You should write "known" and your initials on the face of the check.

5. No. If you think the document has been altered, you should not cash the check. You should ask your supervisor to look at the document. An example of what you might say is, "I need to get this approved by an officer. I'll be right back."

6. No. Anyone could tell you they were related to Mr. Workman. You should ask the customer to show you identification. An example of what you might say is, "Since Mr. Workman isn't with you, does anyone else in the branch know you?" If the customer says no, you should say, "Do you have a piece of ID with your picture on it?"

7. No. These signatures do not match. Notice the different slant, size of letters and shape of letters. You should refer the check to a supervisor. An example of what you might say is, "I need to get this approved. I'll be right back."

8. The ID must have a picture and/or description, a signature, an ID number.

9. Record the issuing agency, the ID number (Remember, you can't write down this number if the ID is a credit card), and the expiration date (if available) on the front of the check.

If you missed any questions, go back and review that section.

Less Cash Deposits – *(continued)*

Here is a chart showing you how to process LESS CASH Transactions. Remember, greet, smile, make eye contact and thank the customer for banking with us all add up to courtesy.

STEP	ACTION
1	Determine that the check is properly endorsed. 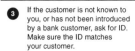
2	Determine if the less cash amount is within your check cashing limits.
3	If the customer is not known to you, or has not been introduced by a bank customer, ask for ID. Make sure the ID matches your customer.
4	Circle the less cash amount. Enter this amount under the date on the deposit slip if space is provided. Have the customer sign on the less cash line in your presence.
5	Process the deposit on TAM. (The next chapter will explain this in more detail and familiarize you with how to use the TAM.)
6	Count out the less cash amount to your customer.
	NOTE: To reduce the chance of paying out the wrong amount, pay the less cash amount indicated on the deposit slip, not from the less cash ticket you created on TAM.
7	Put the deposit slip, less cash ticket and check(s) in POD.
8	Give your customer the transaction record you created on TAM.

This workbook departs from the look of many training materials by using a two-column format and sans serif type for the text.

Reverse type, shading, and icons add visual interest and serve as cues for the reader.

Reverse type is used on the bleeds and on the numbers in Step/Action tables.

A shaded column indicates answers to questions from a progress check that appeared on the preceding page.

Page numbers are in black or white squares in the top outside corner of each page.

Notice the use of a heavy, black sans serif typeface for the headings. This is an easy way to add contrast.

---

chapter thirteen   **105**

Money Orders

The bank offers two types of money orders.

Personal Money Orders are a safe and convenient way for customers to make payments.

International Money Orders are used by customers to send United States funds overseas.

Read the procedures for selling Personal Money Orders and International Money Orders in the Teller Transactions section of the Service Job Aids. Also review the FEES Section of the Service Job Aids.

Progress Check

The purpose of this progress check is to see how well you have learned Money Orders. Answer the questions in the spaces provided. Go back and find answers you don't know.

(7) What is the dollar limit on Personal Money Orders and International Money Orders ?

_____

(8) How do you enter the amount on a money order?

_____

(9) What is the recommended price for an International Money Order?

_____

The correct answers are on the next page.

Travelers Cheques

Customers can purchase Travelers Cheques at your branch.

We do not sell travelers cheques in foreign denominations.

Cheque Packets

Cheques come in packets that contain different amounts in various denominations. The total amount in each packet is shown in large bold figures on the front of each packet. You can only sell these cheques by the packet. They may not be broken; individual cheques may not be sold.

Security

Handle Travelers Cheques as you would cash. Once they are sold, the purchaser uses them in lieu of cash.

NOTE: You should not issue traveler's cheques to non-bank customers if the payment method is by cash in excess of $2,500.00

Sales Advice

Here is a sample of the Sales Advice included with each packet of cheques.

Read the procedures for Selling Travelers Cheques are found in the Travelers Cheques section of the Service Job Aids. You should also review the FEES section of the Service Job Aid.

Read the procedure and answer the following questions.

Software
QuarkXPress

Icons
Created in Illustrator, then converted to a font with Fontographer so each icon can be placed in the document with a keystroke

Forms
Scanned into document, rotated at 5.5%, drop shadow added

Text
Helvetica 10 pt.

Level 1 headings
Helvetica Black 15 pt.

Level 2 headings
Helvetica Black 12 pt.

Answers and cont'd headings
Helvetica Black Italic 9 pt.

Step/Action headings
Helvetica Black and Helvetica 9 pt.

Reverse numbers
Helvetica 10 pt.

Labels on bleed
Helvetica and Helvetica Black 12 pt.

Header
Helvetica 10 pt.

Page numbers
Helvetica Black 12 pt.

Shading
15%

Note: A word processing program may allow you to produce a two-column layout like this, but you'll have less control over the position of elements. The result is not likely to look as refined as it does here.

Example 5

Here are two worksheets from a workbook used in a business writing seminar, before and after their redesign.

Before

These pages need a few simple changes to give them a more sophisticated look and make them more inviting to users.

Breakthrough Business Writing
Reality Check #4 [67]

Reality Check #4

Answer each of these questions in 1 or 2 sentences.

1) What is the most useful or meaningful thing you have learned about grammar so far?

Date

2) What questions remain in your mind at this point?

Date

3) What will be most important for you to learn next?

Date

4) How will you adjust your goals now?

Date

[24]

This format is typical for a business letter. Within organizations, different formats may be required. This format, however, is the basic one that everybody everywhere would understand and accept.

• Tip • Stay on one page

A one page letter has the highest probability of being read. Go to a second page only after serious consideration. Maybe you are trying to cover too much, or the letter is too wordy. Go beyond one page only after you have truly exhausted all possibilities of staying to one page.

• Tip • Be consistent in tone and style

Use the same tone of voice throughout. Shifting from formal to informal or changing point of view (first person to third person, for example) is confusing. If you left justify (the standard), start everything at the left margin and never indent paragraphs. If you indent the date and your signature, indent all the paragraphs.

After

Breakthrough Business Writing   67

Reality Check #4
Answer each of these questions in 1 or 2 sentences.

1) What is the most useful or meaningful thing you have learned about grammar so far?

Date
_____
_____
_____
_____

2) What questions remain in your mind at this point?

_____
_____
_____
_____

3) What will be most important for you to learn next?

_____
_____
_____
_____

4) How will you adjust your goals now?

_____
_____
_____

Putting the page numbers and titles in reverse type in a wide black box adds contrast to each page.

Solid lines look cleaner and less busy than broken lines. White space separates the questions more effectively than does a broken line.

The border around the entire page was removed.

The date only needs to appear once, since all questions are answered at the same time.

Titles and tips look better left-aligned than centered.

24

This format is typical for a business letter. Within organizations, different formats may be required. This format, however, is the basic one that everybody everywhere would understand and accept.

TIP! Stay on one page.

A one page letter has the highest probability of being read. Go to a second page only after serious consideration. Maybe you are trying to cover too much, or the letter is too wordy. Go beyond one page only after you have truly exhausted all possibilities of staying to one page.

TIP! Be consistent in tone and style.

Use the same tone of voice throughout. Shifting from formal to informal or changing point of view (first person to third person, for example) is confusing. If you left justify (the standard), start everything at the left margin and never indent paragraphs. If you indent the date and your signature, indent all paragraphs.

Software
PageMaker
Reverse titles
Helvetica Bold 14 pt.
Text
Times 12 pt.
Reality check heading
Times Bold 18 pt.
Lines
1 pt.

Example 6

This workbook format is used to teach technical product information to entry-level 20- to 26-year-old salespeople. This is an example of basic format 1.

New Technology, New Architecture

Introduction

■ *Features*
• Lorem ipsum dolor sit amet.
• Amet consectetuer.
• Adipiscing elit, sed diam nonummy.
• Nibh euismod tincidunt ut laoreet.

Lorem ipsum dolor sit amet, consectetuer adipiscing elit, sed diam nonummy nibh euismod tincidunt ut laoreet dolore magna aliquam erat volutpat. Ut wisi enim ad minim veniam, quis nostrud exerci tation ullamcorper suscipit lobortis nisl ut aliquip ex ea commodo consequat.

XY Feature: Dolor in hendrerit in vulputate velit esse molestie consequat, vel illum dolore eu feugiat nulla facilisis at vero eros et accumsan et iusto odio dignissim qui blandit praesent luptatum zzril delenit augue duis dolore te feugait nulla facilisi. Lorem ipsum dolor sit amet, consectetuer adipiscing elit, sed diam nonummy nibh euismod tincidunt ut laoreet dolore magna aliquam erat volutpat.

"Always find out if the customer lorem ipsum dolor sit amet."
--Peter Dolor, Sales Mgr.

Ut wisi enim ad minim veniam, quis nostrud exerci tation ullamcorper suscipit lobortis nisl ut aliquip ex ea commodo consequat.

Duis autem vel eum iriure dolor in hendrerit in vulputate velit esse molestie consequat, vel illum dolore eu feugiat nulla facilisis at vero eros et accumsan et iusto odio dignissim qui blandit praesent luptatum zzril delenit augue duis dolore te feugait nulla facilisi.

AB Feature: Nam liber tempor cum soluta nobis eleifend option congue nihil imperdiet doming id quod mazim placerat facer possim assum. Lorem ipsum dolor sit amet, consectetuer adipiscing elit, sed diam nonummy nibh euismod tincidunt ut laoreet dolore magna aliquam erat volutpat.

■ *Key sales tactics*
• Lorem ipsum dolor sit amet.
• Amet consectetuer.
• Lorem ipsum dolor sit amet.

Ut wisi enim ad minim veniam, quis nostrud exerci tation ullamcorper suscipit lobortis nisl ut aliquip ex ea commodo consequat.

Duis autem vel eum iriure dolor in hendrerit in vulputate velit esse molestie consequat, vel illum dolore eu feugiat nulla facilisis at

Sales 2000 Workbook 1

This format works for users who want to get the "big picture" in a hurry.

All the key information is in the left column, in short "word bites" — bullet points, pull quotes, definitions, and brief conceptual overview statements. Small graphics could go in this column as well.

The information is fleshed out in the right column, where users can read the details if they choose.

Software
PageMaker
Title
Helvetica Bold 20 pt., width set at 120%
Text in left column
Helvetica Bold and Normal 10 pt.
Square bullets
Zapf Dingbats 10 pt.
Text in right column
Times 12 pt.
Heading
("Introduction")
Times Bold 16 pt.
Footer
Helvetica Bold Italic 10 pt.
Lines
4 pt. and 1 pt.

8

HANDOUTS

Handouts are the materials you give to participants at a brief presentation, such as a workshop, seminar, or speech.

Handouts usually consist of fewer pages than a workbook and present information in a wider variety of formats. Some handouts are simply reduced views of overhead transparencies or slides; other handouts are not used in the session but are intended only for reference.

If you paged through the handouts from the last class or conference you attended, what would you find? Tiny print on textured paper, where the letters break up and are hard to read? Full pages printed in a script typeface? Pages with long blocks of text and little white space? In each instance the value of the information is diminished by the way it's presented on the page.

Since presenters often use handouts to promote themselves or their businesses, handouts should enhance, not detract from, the presentation.

This chapter shows a variety of formats.

Example 1

The Documentation Series

Data Analysis

Look at the examples on the next page. Lorem ipsum dolor sit amet, consectetuer adipiscing.

- Vel illum dolore eu feugiat nulla facilisis
- Zzril delenit augue duis dolore te feugait nulla
- Facilisis at vero eros et accumsan
- Ut wisi enim ad minim veniam, quis nostrudg
- Dolor in hendrerit

Duis autem vel eum iriure dolor ...

- Ut wisi enim ad minim veniam, quis nostrud:

  - Facilisis at vero
  - Dignissim
  - Nulla facilisi
  - Vulputate
  - Lobortis nisl
  - Illum dolore
  - Aliquam erat
  - Ullamcorper
  - Diam nonummy
  - Nisl ut aliquip
  - Tincidunt

- Ut wisi enim ad minim veniam.
- Vel illum dolore eu feugiat nulla facilisis at vero.

Luptatum zzril delenit augue duis dolore te feugait nulla facilisis eros...

- Vel illum dolore eu feugiat nulla facilisis
- Zzril delenit augue duis dolore te feugait nulla
- Facilisis at vero eros et accumsan
- Ut wisi enim ad minim veniam, quis nostrudg
- Dolor in hendrerit
- Exercitation ullamcorper suscipit lobortis

Keep documents simple. And proofread carefully — details are crucial!

3

Shading, boxes, and a graphic create visual interest on this page.

Plenty of white space makes the page look inviting.

Shading emphasizes the titles printed in bold sans serif type.

Notice how the box shape is repeated. Notice also that the shaded boxes do not have a line border, and the other boxes have single-line borders.

Software
PageMaker

Graphics
Created in PageMaker

Series title
Helvetica Bold Italic
16 pt.

Large title
Palatino 24 pt.; width
set at 80%

Large initial cap
Palatino Bold 36 pt.

Text
Palatino 12 pt.

Headings
Helvetica Bold 13 pt.

Footer
Helvetica Italic 10 pt.

Shading
10%

Example 2

Handout #2

Contact Planning Sheet

Directions: Photocopy this worksheet. Use it to plan your first contact with a new candidate source.

I.   Background Information

Organization _____

Contact Person _____

Position _____

Phone # _____

Referred by _____

II.   Introduction

State your name, position, branch

Purpose of call _____

Determine organization's interest in

referring candidates to you _____

_____

_____

III.   Presentation

Position open/positions we always

need people for _____

_____

_____

Skills/knowledge needed _____

_____

_____

_____

Entry level salary and benefits_____

_____

_____

Hours _____

Benefits of working for us _____

_____

_____

Services we provide to the

community _____

_____

_____

IV.   Ask for Applicants

How best to exchange information
about:

- open positions
  - job descriptions
  - brief overview
- potential candidates
  - resume
  - application

How to:

- arrange interviews
- provide feedback

V.   Follow Up

How best to maintain contact

Next steps _____

_____

_____

_____

_____

Recruiting Clinic 7/93

Headings in reverse type give this worksheet contrast and emphasize the start of each new section.

Since all the text blocks are short, the sans serif type is easy to read.

Repetition is used in two ways: The bars of reverse type are repeated, and the long narrow box in the title repeats the shape of the bars.

To add more space for writing, you could make the type smaller and the margins narrower, thus allowing for slightly longer lines.

Software
Microsoft Word

Title
Helvetica Bold 16 pt.

Text
Helvetica 12 pt.

Reverse headings
Helvetica Bold 12 pt.

Header
Helvetica 12 pt.

Footer
Helvetica 10 pt.

Example 3

Before

Developing a Training Technology Plan

Technology is going to significantly affect training within organizations. It is important to develop a training technology plan to begin or accelerate the process of adapting to this change in order to avoid being overwhelmed in the future.

Some steps to consider. . .

1. Attempt a five-year 'look ahead' to realize the likely impact of technology on your training organization.
  - networks within your organization
  - public networks ('information highway')
  - expectations for multimedia among your users
  - broadcast quality video available on the desktop
  - cheaper, very, very powerful desktop computers
  - cheaper, easier to use authoring tools
  - courseware and training titles widely available for direct purchase by managers

2. Define two or three major phases of implementation that might include:
  - adding multimedia to traditional seminars
  - purchasing off-the-shelf courseware
  - setting platform standards
  - developing customized desktop training internally
  - network-accessed training

3. Each year, budget money (and time) for technology: new hardware, software, courseware, staff training and conferences.

4. Access industry expertise if needed to guide your plans, in order to avoid possible costly mistakes.
  - multimedia
  - networks
  - titles and courseware
  - electronic performance support systems

NSPI 4/21/94   *408-736-2335 Multimedia Training Newsletter*

Here is a page of valuable information, but it's hard to tell what's most important. The title is the same size as the main text in each step, and nothing stands out.

After

Developing a Training Technology Plan

Technology is going to significantly affect training within organizations. It is important to develop a training technology plan to begin or accelerate the process of adapting to this change in order to avoid being overwhelmed in the future.

Some steps to consider. . .

1. **Attempt a five-year 'look ahead' to realize the likely impact of technology on your training organization.**
   - networks within your organization
   - public networks ('information highway')
   - expectations for multimedia among your users
   - broadcast quality video available on the desktop
   - cheaper, very, very powerful desktop computers
   - cheaper, easier to use authoring tools
   - courseware and training titles widely available for direct purchase by managers

2. **Define two or three major phases of implementation that might include:**
   - adding multimedia to traditional seminars
   - purchasing off-the-shelf courseware
   - setting platform standards
   - developing customized desktop training internally
   - network-accessed training

3. **Each year, budget money (and time) for technology: new hardware, software, courseware, staff training and conferences.**

4. **Access industry expertise if needed to guide your plans, in order to avoid possible costly mistakes.**
   - multimedia
   - networks
   - titles and courseware
   - electronic performance support systems

NSPI   4/21/94   408-736-2335 Multimedia Training Newsletter   1

Let's assume this presenter does not want to take the time to create lines, boxes, or shading, or does not know how to do so. Working only with type and using only one typeface, the presenter can still improve the page.

Making the title larger and bold makes it stand out. It's the most important thing on the page.

Boldface type in the steps emphasizes them more than the enlarged type did in the original. And the bold type adds a little bit of contrast.

Hanging indents make the step numbers stand out.

Bullets look better than hyphens in front of the list items, and they too add contrast. The bullets could be indented even further, as in the original.

A page number was added to the footer.

Software
Microsoft Word
Title
Times Bold 22 pt.
Text
Times 13 pt.
Footer
Times Italic 10 pt.

Example 4

Before

Step 1: Reflect

For the next two minutes, reflect on the many things you can do for clients. Think about how you feel after you successfully complete an engagement. Don't make any notes yet!

Step 2: Note Your Ideas

As a consultant I provide the following services/products:	The benefits clients gain from working with me are:
■	■
■	■
■	■
■	■
■	■
■	
■	
■	

My *value-added* servic

- ■
- ■
- ■
- ■
- ■

The design of the worksheet shown on the left is good — big, bold headings, lots of space for writing, and square bullets that add contrast. But the accompanying instructions page lacks visual interest and looks unrelated.

INSTRUCTIONS

Use these guidelines to complete your *Consultant's Action Plan: Defining Yourself.*

Step 1:
Reflect
Take a moment – in fact, take two! Resist the temptation to begin writing. Think about the skills and experiences you bring to a consulting engagement. Remember previous projects that went well. Why? What made them successful? What did you enjoy?

Step 2: Note
Your Ideas
Jot down the services or products clients have bought. Have you written marketing surveys? Developed training manuals? Created strategic plans? List as many products or services as you can.

Next, list the *benefit* the client received from each. Generally, benefits revolve around productivity (better), time (faster), or costs (cheaper).

Where are your competitive advantages? Note extra, value-added services you provide. For example, a safety consultant I met also had 20 years of experience in law enforcement which gave him a unique advantage with clients who required that special expertise. In addition to writing surveys, can you arrange for the interviews? Besides developing training, can you handle all aspects of setting up a

After

Repeating the bold headings on the instructions page ties it and the worksheet together visually. It also makes the instructions page easier to use.

Software
WordPerfect
Headings
Helvetica Bold Italic 16 pt. on instructions, 30 pt. on worksheet
Text
Times 12 pt.

Instructions

Use these guidelines to complete your *Consultant's Action Plan: Defining Yourself.*

Step 1:
Reflect
Take a moment – in fact, take two! Resist the temptation to begin writing. Think about the skills and experiences you bring to a consulting engagement. Remember previous projects that went well. Why? What made them successful? What did you enjoy?

Step 2: Note
Your Ideas
Jot down the services or products clients have bought. Have you written marketing surveys? Developed training manuals? Created strategic plans? List as many products or services as you can.

Next, list the *benefit* the client received from each. Generally, benefits revolve around productivity (better), time (faster), or costs (cheaper).

Where are your competitive advantages? Note extra, value-added services you provide. For example, a safety consultant I met also had 20 years of experience in law enforcement which gave him a unique advantage with clients who required that special expertise. In addition to writing surveys, can you arrange for the interviews? Besides developing training, can you handle all aspects of setting

Example 5

Before

MANAGER'S SKILLS

Lorem ipsum dolor sit amet, consectetuer adipiscing elit

- Sed diam nonummy nibh euismod tincidunt ut laoreet dolore. Magna aliquam erat volutpat.
- Ut wisi enim ad minim
- Veniam quis nostrud
- Exerci tation ullamcorper
- Suscipit lobortis nisl
- Ut aliquip ex ea
- Commodo consequat.

Ut laoreet dolore magna aliquam erat volutpat

Ut wisi enim ad minim veniam, quis nostrud exerci tation. Ullamcorper suscipit lobortis nisl ut aliquip ex ea commodo consequat. Duis autem vel eum iriure dolo

Wisi enim ad mi

Eu feugiat nulla blandit praesen facilisi.

Tation ullamcor

Ut wisi enim ad suscipit lobortis eum iriure dolo

Remember

Don't mix a script typeface such as Tekton or Dom Casual with any other typeface. The Tekton and sans serif used here are too much alike to create either visual interest or contrast.

After

MANAGER'S SKILLS

Lorem ipsum dolor sit amet, consectetuer adipiscing elit

- Sed diam nonummy nibh euismod tincidunt ut laoreet dolore. Magna aliquam erat volutpat.
- Ut wisi enim ad minim
- Veniam quis nostrud
- Exerci tation ullamcorper
- Suscipit lobortis nisl
- Ut aliquip ex ea
- Commodo consequat.

Ut laoreet dolore magna aliquam erat volutpat

Ut wisi enim ad minim veniam, quis nostrud exerci tation. Ullamcorper suscipit lobortis nisl ut aliquip ex ea commodo consequat. Duis autem vel eum iriure dolor in hendrerit in vulputate.

Wisi enim ad minim veniam, quis nostrud exerci tation

Eu feugiat nulla facilisis at vero eros et accumsan et iusto odio dignissim qui blandit praesent luptatum zzril elenit augue duis dolore te feugait nulla facilisi.

Tation ullamcorper

Ut wisi enim ad minim veniam, quis nostrud exerci tation. Ullamcorper suscipit lobortis nisl ut aliquip ex ea commodo consequat. Duis autem vel eum iriure dolor in hendrerit in vulputate.

Remember ad minim veniam, quis nostrud volutpat!

Any script typeface looks best used alone on the page, and used only in very short blocks of text, as shown here.

Software
Microsoft Word
Title
Tekton Bold 30 pt.
Text
Tekton 13 pt.
Headings
Tekton Bold 16 pt.
Shading
10%

Example 6

Many presenters give participants a set of handouts that includes copies of their slides or overheads, printed in a reduced view. Pages 87 and 88 show more examples.

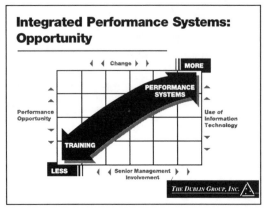

These are color slides that lost very little in their translation to a black and white page.

The heavy, bold type used in the titles projects well on the screen and shows up well on paper. The slides are well designed.

The titles and the company logo are repeated in the same place on each slide.

Software
Persuasion
Graphics
Created in Illustrator
Titles
Franklin Gothic Heavy
40 pt.
Text ("People...")
Palatino Italic 24 pt.

Note: Keep in mind that what looks good on your computer screen may not show up well on paper. Make sure that any critical information on your slides is legible on your handouts.

Example 7

Process for Selecting Team

- Clearly defined knowledge and experience needed

- Clearly defined role and responsibilities

- Asked sponsors

- Explained consequences

HEWLETT PACKARD

Benefits of Selection Approach

- Had right knowledge & skills

- Available at the right time

- For the right amount of time

- With the right motivation

HEWLETT PACKARD

These are reduced views of overhead transparencies designed with lots of white space, one key idea, and only a few lines of text per overhead. They are visually clear and simple.

The designer used a highly legible serif typeface.

Software
Freelance, the graphics package in Lotus Suite
Graphics
SmartPics for Windows clip art
Titles
ITC Century Book 23 pt.
Text
ITC Century Book 16 pt.

Example 8

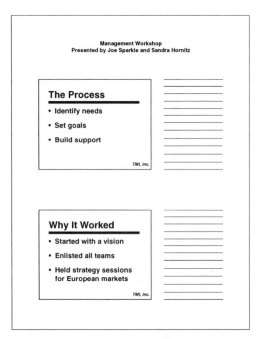

Presentation software such as Persuasion and PowerPoint offers a choice of formats for printing copies of overheads and slides to use as handouts. Pages 86 and 87 showed two formats; here are two more.

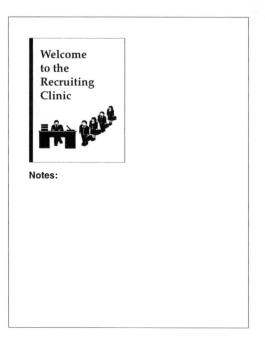

GUIDELINES for overheads and slides

- Use only one typeface. Try using a heavy, black version of the typeface for the titles.

- Use upper- and lower-case letters.

- Use a minimum of 24-point type.

- Show no more than 7 lines of text and 25 characters per line on a slide; showing only 3 to 4 lines is even better.

- Show only one key idea per slide.

- Show only one graphic on a slide.

- Make one visual (a title or graphic) dominant on each slide.

- Number the slides at the bottom.

- Use subtle borders.

INSTRUCTOR GUIDES

An instructor guide (or leader's guide) provides specific directions for teaching a class or leading a workshop. The trainer's personal preferences often dictate the format — some trainers want lots of white space for making notes; others want student materials on the page facing their teaching outline; some want large type so they can read from a distance.

Effective use of graphic design elements can make an instructor guide easier to use. However, a guide does not have to look elegant to be highly functional. Most important is that the format works for the person studying the material or teaching from it.

This chapter shows examples of formats you are likely to recognize. These formats are standard in training materials and have proven effective. However, you may find some new ideas here to increase the usefulness and visual appeal of your instructor guides.

Example 1

This page is from an instructor guide used to train technical trainers.

Module 2: Build Padstack ——————————————— Allegro

2.1 Create Padstack Overview
(10 minutes)
Overhead 2-2

Use OH 2-2 to describe the location of the **PADSTACK** file .pad:

PCBoard → Prep → PADSTACK

Remind students that **PADLIB** is the template, also called a "form", and that they will have to complete this for each Padstack that they create.

Overhead 2-3

Use OH 2-3 to describe the parameters of the **PADLIB** template.

Reference Guide
Pages _____ to _____

Refer students to pages X to X in their Reference Guide to review the parameters of the template.

Ask the students what questions they have about the parameters.

Overhead 2-4

Use OH 2-4 to introduce students to the important commands they will use to create Padstacks.

Student Guide
Page _____

Direct students to read the descriptions of these commands in their Student Guides.

Point out anything special they should note about these commands.

State that you are going to demonstrate how to create a Padstack using the template, parameters and commands just learned.

Rev. 1 ——— 2-4 ——— Valid Logic Systems

Ample white space, lightweight lines, and large sans serif type give this page a clean, open feeling.

References to visual aids and other materials are boxed on the left side of the page. Wide margins within the box create white space so the references are easy to see.

Notice the box is aligned with the lines in the header and footer.

The logo, repeated on every page, identifies a product component and adds a decorative touch.

Software
FrameMaker

Logo
Scanned into document

Text in box
Optima 12 pt.

Heading in box
Optima Bold 14 pt.

Text on right
Optima 14 pt.

Header
Optima Bold 14 pt.

Footer
Optima Italic 10 pt.

Note: Optima is an attractive, readable sans serif typeface, but it is hard to combine effectively with other typefaces. For best results, use it alone, as done here.

Example 2

This page is from an instructor guide used by personnel officers.

Discuss.

- If you are developing a pool of part-time employees, how many will you need in the pool?
- What about other positions for your branch? How many candidates should you know about at any time, whether or not you have a specific opening?
- What other questions/concerns do you have about your recruiting responsibilities?

2. Applicant Pool Exercise (15 min.)

Handout #1: Applicant Pool Exercise Worksheet.

- Let's do an exercise to help us identify a major recruiting issue: where to find candidates.
- When we finish, we'll share our ideas so you'll each leave with a list of places to investigate for candidates.
- Take a minute to read the directions on the handout.

**OH 7
Paraphrase directions.**

Assign groups.

- Do you have any questions?

Provide chart paper, masking tape and markers to each group.

Do exercise. Allow 10 minutes.

Chart responses.

- Let's quickly hear from each group about the sources you shared that were most valuable.
- Now review all the lists and select at least three new sources for candidates that you will research for your branch.

Discuss results.

Transition: Now that we've built a recruiting foundation, let's look at how to effectively approach new sources for candidates.

Recruiting Clinic

3

In the left-hand column, boldface text and symbols give directions for activities and provide references to handouts and visuals. "OH" refers to overhead.

The text on the right-hand side of the page is a script for the trainer.

A sans serif typeface is appropriate here because there are no long lines or blocks of text.

Software
Microsoft Word
Graphics
Created in Word's graphics window
Text in left column
Helvetica Bold 12 pt.
Text in right column
Helvetica 12 pt.
Footer
Helvetica 12 pt.

Example 3

This is a template page for an instructor guide.

Time	Activity	Content	Materials
10 minutes	**Lecture**	**Topic Title** 1. Introduce lorem ipsum dolor sit amet, consectetuer adipiscing elit, sed diam nonummy. 2. Explain enim ad minim veniam, quis nostrud exerci tation ullamcorper suscipit lobortis nisl ut aliquip ex ea commodo consequat. 3. Ask consectetuer adipiscing elit, sed diam nonummy.	Welcome to the XYZ Class
20 minutes	**Group Activity**	**Activity Title** 1. Introduce autem vel eum iriure dolor in hendrerit in vulputate velit esse molestie. 2. Point out nulla facilisis at vero eros et accumsan et iusto odio dignissim. 3. Explain nulla facilisis at vero eros et accumsan et iusto odio dignissim qui blandit praesent luptatu. 4. Ask odio dignissim qui blandit praesent luptatum zzril delenit augue duis dolore te feugait nulla facilisi. 5. Allow nulla facilisis at vero eros et accumsan et iusto odio dignissim qui blandit praesent luptatum zzril delenit. 6. Debrief dignissim qui blandit praesent luptatum zzril delenit augue duis dolore te feugait nulla facilisi.	XYZ Series
10 minutes	**Individual Work**	**Exercise Title** 1. Explain autem vel eum iriure dolor in hendrerit in vulputate velit esse molestie. 2. Ask lorem ipsum dolor sit amet, consectetuer adipiscing elit, sed diam nonummy. 3. Give odio dignissim qui blandit praesent luptatum zzril delenit augue duis dolore te feugait nulla facilisi. 4. Ask duis autem vel eum iriure dolor in hendrerit in vulputate velit esse molestie consequat, vel illum dolore eu feugiat nulla facilisis.	XYZ Series

Workshop Instructor Guide   1

Large numbers and shading in the left column call attention to the time frames. This format is useful when it's critical that the instructor stay on schedule.

Icons indicate the type of learning activity.

A reduced view of overheads is in the right-hand column.

A thin line separates the activities.

Software
Microsoft Word
Graphics
Icons created in Word's graphics window; overheads imported from Persuasion
Column headings
Helvetica Bold 14 pt.
Text and titles
Palatino and Palatino Bold 11 pt.
Large numbers
Palatino 24 pt.
Labels on icons
Helvetica Bold 11 pt.
Footer
Helvetica Bold 10 pt.
Shading
10%

Example 4

This page is from an instructor guide used in a strategic planning session.

Strategic Planning   1-1

Section 1: Introduction

Purpose	**Steps**
• To explain the purpose of the session	1. Welcome participants.
• To provide background on why the session was scheduled	2. Explain purpose.
	3. Describe objectives.
• To identify participants' responsibilities in the session	4. Present agenda.
	5. Explain ground rules.
	6. Conduct "Jump Start" activity.

8:30 – 8:45
(15 min)

1. Welcome participants.

Welcome participants and introduce yourself.

OT 1

Have participants introduce themselves, following the guidelines on the overhead.

2. Explain purpose.

● You have been invited to this session to help determine and clarify your role in the planning process. You have been invited to this session to help determine and clarify your role in the planning process. You have been invited to this session to help determine and clarify your role in the planning process. You have been invited to help determine and clarify your role.

OT 2, Page 1

Ask participants to complete the exercise on Page 1 of their handout materials. Ask for several volunteers to read their responses to the whole group.

OT 3, Page 2

3. Describe objectives.

Leader's Guide 2/15/95

On the first page of each section, the purpose and steps are summarized in two columns at the top of the page. They are in a smaller point size.

A heavy line emphasizes the title; thin lines divide the page into sections.

Each step appears in boldface in the teaching outline.

A big bullet and a larger point size indicate paragraphs that are intended as a script for the trainer.

Software
Microsoft Word

Section title
New Century Schoolbook Bold 15 pt.

Text
New Century Schoolbook 12 pt.; purpose and steps 10 pt.; trainer script 14 pt.

Large bullet
Zapf Dingbats 14 pt.

Header
New Century Schoolbook Bold 12 pt.

Footer
New Century Schoolbook Italic 10 pt.

Example 5

These two pages are from an instructor guide in an award-winning program that teaches production management skills to customer service managers.

OUTLINE   **Module 6**

TIME	WORKBOOK PAGE	OUTLINE	VISUALS
ST 1:35 BL 40 min		7. Planning Exercise (Part 1)*	
		- Purpose: To begin planning the project and to present the project plan to other participants for feedback	
	6-10	- Participants read instructions	
		- Summarize instructions	**10** Instructions
		- Check understanding	
(30 min)		- Participants work alone	
ST 2:15 BL 30 min		8. Planning Exercise (Part 2)*	
		- Assign groups	
		- Explain presentation process	
		- Participants present within small groups	
ST 2:45 BL 15 min		BREAK	
ST 3:00 BL 20 min		9. Planning Exercise (Part 3)*	
		- Debrief Create "hot list"	
		- Reminder: Buddy system	
		- Participants complete Project Planner to leave with instructor	
		TRANSITION: You've now completed Step 2 of your project. Let's see what happens in Steps 3 and 4.	

LEADER'S GUIDE   6 - 4

This page is from the teaching outline portion of the guide.

Each step in the outline is separated by a thin line.

The "Visuals" column lists titles of overheads and prepared flip charts.

Even though the print is small, there is lots of white space. Wide space between columns makes the references to workbook pages and visuals easy to find.

REFERENCE   Module 6

OUTLINE STEP NUMBER	OUTLINE TOPIC

5   **Overview of project planning process**

Explain that participants will use two forms they learned how to use in Day 2 -- the Strategy Planner and the Presentation Planner. They also need to use a Project Planner. Review the job aid for filling out the Project Planner.

Tell participants that if it is geographically possible, they must team up with another Service Manager to give and receive feedback on their implementation activities. At least once during the project, they should visit the office of another Service Manager to discuss and review progress on the post-course project.

6   **How to complete the project**

Explain that to complete the project, participants will gather and analyze data, using all the tools they have been introduced to in this program. Review the job aids on pages 6-8 and 6-9 in the workbook.

Managers will also need to develop recommendations, which will require making decisions about what actions to take based on the results of the data gathering and analysis.

7, 8, 9   **Planning Exercise**

       Purpose: To begin planning the project and to make a 5-minute presentation describing the plan.

       Time: 10 minutes introducing exercise
                    30 minutes working alone
                    30 minutes presenting in small groups
                    15 minutes debriefing
                    <u>05 minutes preparing Project Planner</u>
                    90 minutes total

This page is from the reference section, which contains important background reading and detailed instructions for exercises.

The numbers in the left-hand column correspond to the step numbers in the teaching outline.

Software
Ventura Publisher
Text
Times 10 pt.
Column headings
Helvetica Bold 10 pt.
Header
Helvetica Bold 12 pt.
Footer
Helvetica 8 pt.

Example 6

These Before and After pages are from an instructor guide used to teach financial product information to new employees.

Before

Corporate Bonds

❏ Straight
❏ Convertible
❏ Callable

→ *("Corporate Bonds" Slide).*
→ Priced in fractions - for example 101.1/8 = 1,011.25.

→ Three basic types:

→ 1. Straight - no features.

→ 2. Convertible - privilege of converting the bond into a specified number of common shares at any time. The number received is called the conversion ratio.

→ 3. Callable - the bond can be redeemed prior to maturity at the issuers discretion.

Securities Exercise (30 Minutes)

✓ Securities exercise - Securities Handout

> Divide participants into several groups. There are seven securities. Ideally there should be about five people in each group. Have them answer the questions on the handout. Give them about 10 minutes. Question each group about the security by using the handout. The time and involvement of answers determines the number of questions asked.

Review of Objectives

✓ Give a description of a Corporation:

→ 1. It is regarded by our legal system as distinct and apart from its owners.
→ 2. It may own property; it can incur debt.
→ 3. It can sue and be sued.
→ 4. It has perpetual life; limited liability.

✓ List two ways a corporation can raise money:
→ Fund debt (bonds)
→ Issue stock

Mutual Funds - Leader's Guide   6   *Human Resources - Training & Development*

This guide is well organized, and each type style and symbol is a cue for an activity. But too many symbols and varieties of type make the page look busy and confusing.

This is the key used:

✔ = *say or do to introduce a topic.*

→ = *say about a topic.*

Box = *note to trainer, not to be read to class.*

Outline font = *handouts.*

After

This version looks simpler and easier to use.

The new key is:

Bold type = *topics the trainer should cover; points indented under bold type are things the trainer should say.*

(Boldface italics)
= slides and handouts.

■ *= an exercise.*

Box = *note to trainer* (as before, but the box has a lighter, less busy border).

Software
WordPerfect
Text
Bookman 12 pt.
Headings
Bookman Bold and Bold Italic 12 pt.
Footer
Helvetica Bold Italic 10 pt.

Corporate Bonds
- ☐ Straight
- ☐ Convertible
- ☐ Callable

(Corporate Bonds Slide)

Priced in fractions - for example 101.1/8 = 1.011.25.

Three basic types:

1. Straight – no features.
2. Convertible – privilege of converting the bond into a specified number of common shares at any time. The number received is called the conversion ratio.
3. Callable – the bond can be redeemed prior to maturity at the issuer's discretion.

Securities Exercise (30 minutes)

■ **Securities exercise - *(Securities Handout)***

Divide participants into several groups. There are seven securities. Ideally there should be about five people in each group. Have them answer the questions on the handout. Give them about 10 minutes. Question each group about the security by using the handout. The time and involvement of answers determines the number of questions asked.

Review of Objectives

Give a description of a Corporation:

1. It is regarded by our legal system as distinct and apart from its owners.
2. It may own property: it can incur debt.
3. It can sue and be sued.
4. It has perpetual life: limited liability.

List two ways a corporation can raise money:

1. Fund debt (bonds)
2. Issue stock

Example 7

This page is from an instructor guide used to teach principles of self-governance to leaders of nongovernmental organizations in developing nations.

Recognizing Self-Governing Organizations   **5**

CUES	DETAILED NOTES

Learning Map

Refer participants to the Module 5 block on the Workshop Learning Map located in their Participant's Workbook.

> **What does self-governance look like in action?**

Introduce Module 5 by explaining that in this module participants will be using the eight design tools to determine whether an organization is self-governing or not.

Note: You may assign the Sri Lankan Fishery Story and Update to be read as homework the night before. If you do, be sure to cover steps 2 and 3 of the Preparation instructions when you make this homework assignment.

Learning Activity #1

SRI LANKAN FISHERY STORY (50 minutes)
(Small Group Activity)

Preparation: (5 minutes)

1. Divide participants into small groups of 3-5 persons each.

   Note: The groups should be different than those identified in Module 4.

PW p# _____

2. Refer participants to the Activity Assignment Sheet located in Module 5 of their Participant's Workbook, and review this information.

3. Explain that after groups complete the assignment, they will report their findings to the large group.

© 1994 ICS   Facilitator's Guide 1.0   5-2

The module number in reverse type at the top and the shaded bar used to highlight column headings give this page a bit of contrast.

The "Cues" column refers to classroom activities and participant workbook (PW) page numbers.

The text is in a large point size because trainers want to be able to read it from a distance.

Software
Microsoft Word

Text
Palatino 14 pt.

Column headings
Helvetica Bold 14 pt.

Headings in left column
Helvetica Bold 12 pt.

Header
Helvetica Bold 12 pt.; number is 18 pt.

Footer
Helvetica Bold 10 pt.

Shading
20%

10
JOB AIDS

Job aids are convenient reference tools that provide information when people need it. Quick reference cards, "cheat sheets," task checklists, and user guides are all examples of job aids.

Job aids often provide summaries or reminders of what was taught in a class or learned from a workbook. For example, a salesperson who studied a workbook to learn about a product might carry a datebook-sized checklist of questions to refer to when meeting with a customer.

Sometimes a job aid is a substitute for training. Employees may not need to take a class or study a subject — they just need to have information available in an easily accessible format so they can look something up when they need it. Pulling the key information out of a thick manual that frustrates users and turning it into a job aid, for example, often solves problems and makes a task easier.

Job aids are often designed in a small size convenient to carry or store next to a computer. Their size restrictions can present a challenge — how do you fit all the information into the format? Whether wallet size or poster size, job aids can be both functional and attractive. This chapter shows a range of formats.

Example 1

These pages are from a small booklet summarizing key points in a supervisory training program.

DELEGATION

▲ Make the "critical jump" to managing rather than doing.

▲ Delegate authority equal to the employee's responsibility.

▲ What to delegate — anything that is not a true managerial function. Do not delegate:
   • Planning
   • Policy making
   • Goal setting
   • Budgeting
   • Confidential and personnel matters

▲ To whom to delegate —
   and available, who will
   assignment, and who c

▲ Delegate at the level yo
   less mature employees.
   experienced and compe
   control.

Management Training

GIVING FEEDBACK

▲ If you want others to understand you, you must first demonstrate that you understand them.

▲ Give feedback about *behavior* (not attitudes). Look for opportunities to give positive as well as negative feedback.

   • Give positive feedback immediately after the behavior. Give negative feedback immediately, but make sure you are detached enough to feel in control.
   • Feedback should be specific, not personal. Use it to solve problems, not to judge and blame.

▲ Key: Ask questions rather than make statements or accusations.

▲ Steps:
   1. Briefly describe the problem.
   2. Listen and summarize.
   3. Give your point of view and show that the problem is worth solving.
   4. Discuss possible solutions.
   5. Obtain commitments and timelines for change.
   6. Offer your encouragement and help.

American Training Systems

This is a simple layout with lots of white space and high contrast.

Reverse type in a black box highlights the title on each page and makes it easy to find a topic.

The sans serif type looks clean and simple.

Bold triangles used as bullets make each key point stand out. The triangle is also repeated in a larger size as a graphic in the page number.

The bold line at the bottom of the page repeats the look of the black box at the top.

Software
PageMaker

Reverse titles
Helvetica Bold 14 pt.

Text
Helvetica 12 pt.

Triangle bullets
Zapf Dingbats 12 pt.

Page numbers
Helvetica Bold 16 pt. on a Zapf Dingbats 30-pt. triangle

Footer
Helvetica Italic 9 pt.

Line
6 pt.

Page size
5 1/2" x 8 1/2"

Example 2

This booklet was created on standard 8 1/2-by-11-inch pages, then printed in the size shown here.

How to Use This Pocket Guide

Four symbols are used in the pocket guide. Each is described below.

 These pages 'point out' specific information about the tools, methods and procedures of quality improvement.

 'Job aids' are guides, tables and charts that provide specific directions on using the methods and tools of quality improvement.

 These pages 'summarize' key points. They are found at the end of each chapter.

 This symbol is meant to 'remind' you of important information. They are usually found on each summary page.

The pag...
Manage...
the pag...
will be...
Manage...

Critical Requirement	Unit Measure...
timeliness	% of 'bills

Software
PageMaker

Graphics
T/Maker ClickArt clip art

Titles
Palatino Bold 12 pt.

Text
Palatino 10 pt.

Page numbers
Avant Garde Bold 10 pt.

Page size
3 7/8" x 5 1/2"

 Measurement Systems   CSM-30

Before you measure a process, you need to identify the parameters in which measurement (and the subsequent analysis) will occur. The example below descr...
of a typical 'accounts...

JOB AID **Performance Cues**   CSM-31

Observable cues in the work environment can suggest that a quality improvement effort...

PERFORMANCE CUE	CON...
Activities u... incoming ... *mistakes of* ...	
rework	

 Methods - Summary   CSM-84

There are many methods and techniques available to help your quality improvement efforts. Selecting the right one(s) requires pinpointing the source of the problem or opportunity for improvement. Then the most appropriate method(s) can be identified, developed, implemented and evaluated.

➤ Pinpoint the cause of the problem or opportunity before you expend resources to develop and implement any method(s) of improvement.

➤ Use common sense when selecting improvement methods. Consider available budget and how receptive the work environment will be to the type

---

The graphic symbols explained on this "How To Use" page are repeated throughout the guide. They are always on the left side of the page.

The graphics are simple, clear, and consistent in style. The page number is in a contrasting typeface.

Example 3

This is a segment from a scheduling tool, shown at actual size.

Operator Schedule

July 1995	1 S	2 S	3 M	4 T	5 W	6 Th	7 F
Lisa Schneider	☀	☀				☀	☀
Sam Ellis	☀	☀				☀	☀
Alison Reale			☀	☀	☀		
Marty Lipscomb			☀	☀	☀		
Paul Devlin	○	○				○	○
Carolina Flanders	○	○				○	○
Rick Cockran			○	○	○		
Mandy Davis			○	○	○		

☀ Day Shift: 7 AM - 7 PM
○ Night Shift: 7 PM - 7 AM

Creative use of simple graphic symbols resulted in a job aid that is visually interesting and easy to understand.

The sun and moon symbols indicate day and night shifts; shading indicates days an operator does not work.

Software
Excel
Symbols
Zapf Dingbats 18 pt.
Title
Helvetica Bold 14 pt.
All other type
Helvetica 10 pt.
Shading
Light gray

These pages are from a software user guide.

Example 4

General Techniques for the Host Terminal Training Window

Topic	How do I...	Procedure
Unidentified	See a complete host screen if only part is displayed.	If the host pauses, ScreenRead may show an incomplete screen labeled Unidentified. Click on Refresh when host is ready.
Freeze Refresh	Stop a screen from being continuously updated.	Check the box labeled Freeze Screen to stop continuous screen updating. When Freeze Screen box is checked, the screen is refreshed only when you click on Refresh.
Screen Details	See details about the current screen.	Double-click on Screen Name to see Screen Definition Detail window (use Windows menu if window gets lost). Click on Details to see more about selected identifier. To delete selected label or branch, click on Delete.
Off-Line Training	Train screens without being connected to a host computer.	In Select Host Session window (StartHost): Click on Disconnect. Host Terminal Training window: Train screens that were been identified on-line. Click on Next to record keys to get to next screen. Click on Stop after recording keys; choose next screen from Select A Screen window. Use Select Host Session window to re-connect for on-line training.

Agent Terminal

Special Data Fields in DefineFields Step

Topic	How do I...	Procedure
Relative Fields	Make a field's position relative to something else.	Mark field on screen; double-click on it; click on Relative. Indicate what it's relative to (cursor, another field, read marker, etc.).
Read Marker	Make a field's position relative to the read marker.	In the UseTerminal step: *Get* read marker location to copy row and column to integer objects. *Set* read marker location to row and column contained in integer objects. In DefineFields: Read marker is shown as red arrow if fields are relative to it. You can drag arrow to *simulate* UseTerminal step for training, but you must use UseTerminal to set read marker when job description is run.

23

Mailbox Steps

For more details, see the manual titled
Introduction to the Agent Trainer.

Action/Device	Icon	Description	Notes
Start Mailbox	StartMailbox	Trigger Step: Starts a software agent running a job description when it receives data sent to the mailbox by another agent or an administrator.	Create the StartMailbox job description *first*. Create fields to hold data sent to mailbox.
Send Mailbox	SendMailbox	Sends data to the mailbox. Copies data from objects to the fields in the mailbox.	To train: Enter name of the StartMailbox job description; copy objects to its fields.
Update Mailbox	UpdateMailbox	Changes contents of mailbox so software agent gets different data when restarting a job description that could not be completed (e.g. puts an alternate fax number in mailbox if first number failed).	This step can be used only in job descriptions that begin with StartMailbox and are set to Restart in the StopFlow step.

The next pages present a *few* uses
for the Calculator. See the *Introduction
to the Agent Trainer* for more.

The Calculator Step

Action/Device	Icon	Description	Notes
Convert Calc	ConvertCalc	Allows software agent to process data: • Add, subtract, multiply, divide, and other functions such as percentage, absolute value • Manipulate text strings, phone numbers, times, dates • Convert data from one type to another or force results to be a certain data type	To copy data from one type of object to a different type: 1. Place object name in Expression. 2. Place new object in Put the Results In... and enter type when asked to create object.

28

Times and Helvetica are combined here in an interesting way.

The serif titles are not bold, but they stand out because they are much larger than the text and have a light line under them. The page numbers are even larger.

Narrow sans serif type in the column headings and on the bleed allows more letters to fit in the small space available.

Lines (not busy boxes) frame each section.

The bleed and light shading add contrast.

Software
Word for Windows
Graphics
Created in Paintbrush, a Windows application
Titles
Times Italic 16 pt.
Text
Times 9 pt.
Headings
Helvetica Narrow Bold 9 pt.
Page numbers
Times Italic 30 pt.
Shading
10%
Page size
8 1/2" x 5 1/2"

Example 5

This is a quick reference card to help users understand a complex receivables mainframe software application.

IHFS

QUICK

REFERENCE

CARD

(Updated 11/91)

Type Commands

i ....invoices
c ....credits
d ....debits

Age Commands

c ....current due items
f ....future due items
p ....past due items

Status Commands

p ....POD
d ....disputed
a ....age override

Show Commands

po..............purchase order (default)
cocli ....company/client
rsn.............reason code
checkno ...check number
id ....user id (posted)
selid ....user id (selected)
disca ....discount amount
xref ....cross ref number
xrefdt ....cross ref date
str ....store id
cf ....customer ref number
dispdt ....dispute date
batchdt .....batch date
batchno.....batch number
sbatchdt....selected
sbatchno...selected
ocno ....order cntrl number
cprno.........cpr number
chk ....full check amount
rep..............sales rep
origdt ....original date
chgddt ....date of change

Sequence Commands

tc ....transaction code
              (default)
fdue ....final due date
cf ....customer reference
              number
amt ....dollar amount
str...............store
po ....purchase order number
inv ....invoice
openitem...checks in process
c _____...split accounts
rsn ....reason code

Suspend/Transfer Commands

b ....basic data
c ....credit data
su ....a/r summary
oi ....a/r open items
ci ....a/r closed items
aa ....a/r account aging
cd ....credit decision

(PF10 to return to original screen)

Closed Item Commands

(select type)
ck ....check number
je ....j/e number
cd ....closing date
ci ....closed invoice
cf ....customer ref
       number
tr ....transfer
zb ....zero bal. corr.
od ....open item deleted
ec ....equals clean-off

Closed Type Commands

p ......posted items
i ......invoices
c ......credits
d ......debits

Customer Select Commands (PF13)

sn ....short name
rf .....invoice number
as ....elesco number
ac ....brittania number
cg ....split account
mn ...MICR number

Lots of white space helps give this job aid a clean, uncluttered look. The reverse titles and the bold type used for the commands add contrast.

The serif typeface is clear and readable; the sans serif on the labels provides a type contrast.

Too many dotted lines can make a page look busy, but here they are okay because the lines are short.

Software
PageMaker
Title
Helvetica Italic 16 pt.
Reverse labels
ITC Stone Sans
9 pt.
Commands
Bookman and
Bookman Bold 9 pt.
Page size
4 1/4" x 11"

Note: If you want to duplicate this look, use only one sans serif typeface. Don't combine two sans serifs on the same page.

Example 6

These pages are from a small booklet of equipment operating instructions.

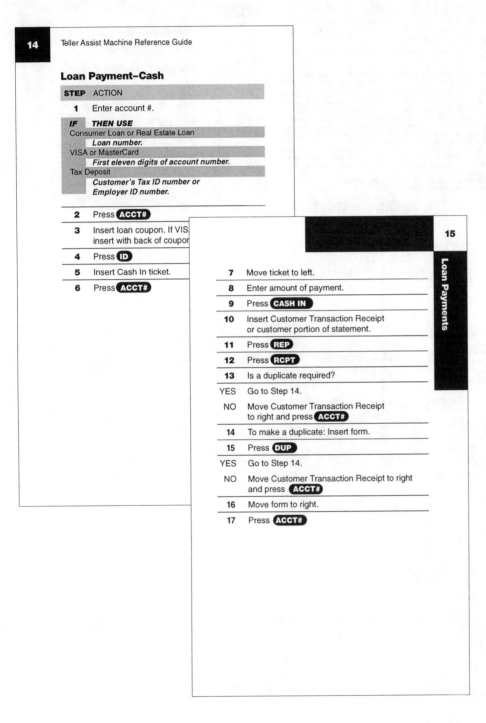

Reverse type on the oval key labels and in the section title (on the bleed) creates contrast.

The page number is in a black or white square in the outer corner of each page.

A shaded bar signals the Step/Action format; the "If" information in the table is also shaded. The bold step numbers stand out clearly.

Light lines separate the steps; notice there are no vertical lines.

Software
QuarkXPress

Text
Helvetica 10 pt.

Headings
Helvetica Black 12 pt.

Step/Action headings
Helvetica Black and
Helvetica 9 pt.

If/Then headings
Helvetica Black and
Helvetica Black Italic 9 pt.

Step numbers
Helvetica Black 10 pt.

Oval labels
Helvetica Black 9 pt.;
ovals drawn in Quark

Label on bleed
Helvetica Black 11 pt.

Header
Helvetica 9 pt.

Page numbers
Helvetica Black 11 pt.

Page size
4 1/4" x 7"

Example 7

This page is from a financial services product manual. The After example shows the redesign of the numerical information on the Before page.

Before

This is an example of a low-contrast page. Despite the amount of white space, the page does not look inviting or easy to use. It's hard to tell what's important because nothing stands out.

PROGRAM REQUIREMENTS (continued)

Secondary Financing (Continued)
- If NORTH AMERICAN MORTGAGE COMPANY® is refinancing a first with Subordinate Financing to be left in place, the Subordinate Financing must meet the above standards and the existing junior lien must be subordinated to the new refinance first.
- If subordinate financing is a fixed rate second lien, and the sum of the *original* balances of the first and second mortgages exceeds FNMA and FHLMC maximum loan limits, then we must have written verification from the second lender that the second will not be or has not been sold to FNMA or FHLMC. Written verification isn't necessary when the second is an equity line of credit since FNMA and FHLMC don't purchase them.
- ⋙ On FNMA 95% No Cash Out refinances, no secondary financing may be involved. This includes paying off or subordinating existing secondary financing.
- On FHLMC 95% No Cash Out refinances, no secondary financing may be paid off. Existing secondary financing may be subordinated to the new first lien if the new loan to value is not in excess of 75% and the combined loan to value does not exceed 95%.

Loan To Value
- On-purchase, value is the lower of the sale price or appraised value.
- On refinances, value is current appraised value.

Property Type	Loan Type	Max LTV Without Secondary Financing	Max LTV of first with Secondary Financing	Max CLTV
Owner Occupied 1 Family, SFD, Condo, PUD	Purchase:	95%	75%	90%
	No Cash Out Refi:	90%	75%	90%
	Cash Out Refi:	75%	75%	75%
	Purchase (FHLMC Only)	N/A	80%	90%
	No Cash Out Refi (FHLMC Only)	N/A	80%	90%
⋙	No Cash Out Refi (FNMA Only)	95%	N/A	N/A
	No Cash Out Refi (FHLMC Only)	95%	N/A	N/A
Owner Occupied 2 Family	Purchase:	90%	75%	90%
	No Cash Out Refi:	90%	75%	90%
	Cash Out Refi:	75%	75%	75%
	Purchase (FHLMC Only)	N/A	80%	90%
	No Cash Out Refi (FHLMC Only)	N/A	80%	90%
Owner Occupied 3-4 Family	Purchase:	80%	75%	80%
	No Cash Out Refi:	75%	75%	75%
	Cash Out Refi:	75%	75%	75%
Second Homes 1 Family Only SFD, Condo, PUD	Purchase:	80%	75%	90%
	No Cash Out Refi:	75%	70%	70%
	Cash Out Refi: (FNMA only)	65%	N/A	N/A
	Purchase (FHLMC Only)	90%	75%	90%
	No Cash Out Refi (FHLMC Only)	80%	70%	70%
Investor 1-4 Family SFD, Condo, PUD	Purchase:			
	1-2 Family	70%	70%	70%
	3-4 Family	60%	60%	70%
	No Cash Out Refi:			
	1-2 Family	70%	70%	70%
	3-4 Family	60%	60%	70%
1-2 Family (No Condo's)	Cash Out Refi: (FHLMC only)	65%	N/A	N/A

See additional refinance restrictions (page 7 and 8).

Note: Except as noted, the above LTV's are for generic loans. Other loan types have different LTV's and loan parameters, as explained elsewhere in this announcement. These include, for example, non-permanent resident aliens, financed MIP loans, FNMA-Only semi-annual buydowns, FHLMC-Only 80/10/10, and FHLMC-Only higher second home LTV's, FNMA-Only second home Cash Out refis, and FHLMC-Only Cash Out investor refis.

REVISED
February 10, 1994

30/20/15 YEAR CONFORMING FIXED
H01, H04, H07, H09 / H06 / H20, H21, H08, H10

PAGE 5 of 18
103WLP.H01

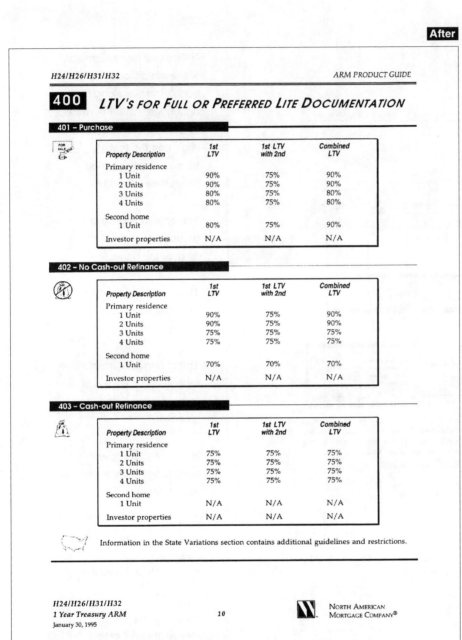

After

Reverse type and boxes are used effectively in this version and add contrast.

The boxes have a subtle drop shadow that repeats the look of the bold lines at the top and bottom of the page.

Two line weights are used; the heavier line signals the beginning and end of a section.

Software
Microsoft Word

Graphics
For Sale sign created in Illustrator; others are clip art

Title
Avant Garde Bold and Italic 18 pt.; number is expanded 3 pts.; text is small caps

Text
Palatino 10 pt.

Reverse headings
Avant Garde Bold 10 pt.

Headings in boxes
Helvetica Narrow Bold Italic 10 pt.

Header
Palatino Italic 10 pt.

Footer
Palatino Bold 10 pt.

Lines
2 pt. and hairline

Page size
8 1/2" x 11"

Note: It is preferable not to mix two sans serif typefaces, even though they are far apart as on this page. If you want to create this look, use only one.

Example 8

This page is from a software user guide.

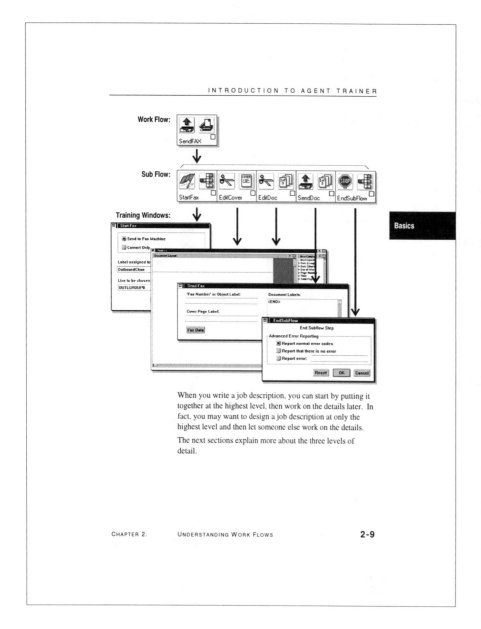

Notice that three elements are aligned along the left edge, and five along the right edge. Also, the rows of icons, the third screen shot, and the text paragraph are aligned along their left edges.

The screen shots are grouped neatly, not spread all over the page.

The bleed and the black and shaded areas in the screens add contrast.

The rectangular shape is repeated in the rows of icons, screens, and the bleed.

Plenty of white space adds to the attractiveness of this page.

Software
Word for Windows
Graphics
Screen shots laid out in CorelDRAW!
Text
Times Roman 11 pt.
Headings and bleed
Helvetica Narrow Bold 10 pt.
Header
Helvetica 8 pt.
Footer
Helvetica 8 pt., small caps
Page number
Helvetica Bold 12 pt.
Page size
7" x 9"

Example 9

This quick reference card explains how to operate a scale that weighs money. It is the same size as the operating manual.

How to Use the K-Scale: Quick-Reference Steps

If you have never used the scale before, read other side first.

1 *Turn the scale on.*

2 *Press [↑] or [↓] to set denomination and [→] to set currency type:*

CURRENCY	ROLLED COIN	LOOSE COIN
Set to proper currency denomination and currency type.	Set to **any currency** denomination.	Set to **coin** denomination. Display will say SCOOP ON. Put scoop on platform.

3 *Place items on the platform:*

CURRENCY	ROLLED COIN	LOOSE COIN
• Loose bills in handfuls up to the maximum. • Straps or clips, one at a time.	One roll at a time. You may mix denominations on the platform. You may count rolled coin and currency at the same time.	In handfuls up to the maximum.

- The active counter displays the dollar amount on the platform.
- The scale BEEPS when it has counted the items.
- If the scale BUZZES, there is a problem with the last item set on the platform. See the Buzz Chart on the other side of this page.

4 *You can place as much currency or coin on the platform as it will hold. If the platform is full and:*

- You want to continue to count more currency or coin, simply clear the platform and keep counting.
  OR
- You want to get a total of the items you are counting, press [+]. The accumulator will show the current accumulated total. **You must always press [+] before clearing the platform.** (If you are done adding totals, press [C] to clear the accumulator). You may now count more currency or coin.

Black bars along the left edge provide contrast and draw attention to the step numbers in reverse type. The shaded area behind each step also adds contrast.

Text printed over the shading is in bold sans serif type. The text in the white boxes is serif.

The boldface italics used in the instructions is readable because it is used only in small amounts and the shading behind it is very light.

Software
PageMaker
Title
Helvetica Bold 18 pt.
Text
Palatino 11 pt.
Headings in steps
Helvetica Bold Italic
12 pt.
Step numbers
Helvetica Bold Italic
18 pt.
Shading
10%
Page size
7" x 8 1/2"

Example 10

This job aid is used in the financial services industry to train system users.

Before

<u>GateKeeper PegaSHARES Entry Job Aid</u>

<u>Objectives:</u>

- To determine if a case has been entered on Pegashares on correspondence recieved in good order in the service areas.   (Step A)
- To determine if the entered case is active or resolved.   (Step B)
- To enter and transfer a new case if no case exists.   (Step C)

<u>Given:</u>

- The Administrative Assistant has completed a two day, eight hour course in GateKeeper/PegaSHARES, knows how to log on/log off the system and the major key functions.
- The Administrative Assistant knows how to find an account number in SunGard.

<u>Step A: Does a case exist?</u>

- Display the Command Screen.
- Type ˙ Action: IFND
         P1:   Fund NumberAccount Number

<u>Step B: Existing Case:</u>

- Is the existing case resolved?
    If **Yes**:
          attach Routing Slip to correspondence and forward to Operator (Rep).
    If **Not**: (see back)

Customer Service Administration Technical Training Department
PegaSHARES Gatekeeper Course, Job Aid

Double underlining in the title looks busy and is not the best choice for emphasis on this one-page job aid.

Lack of space between bullet items, and lack of hanging indents, make the instructions look cramped.

After

GateKeeper PegaSHARES Entry Job Aid

Objectives:

- To determine if a case has been entered on Pegashares on correspondence received in good order in the service areas. (Step A)

- To determine if the entered case is active or resolved.   (Step B)

- To enter and transfer a new case if no case exists.   (Step C)

Given:

- The Administrative Assistant has completed a two day, eight hour course in GateKeeper/PegaSHARES, knows how to log on/log off the system and the major key functions.

- The Administrative Assistant knows how to find an account number in SunGard.

Step A: Does a case exist?

- Display the Command Screen.

- Type   Action: IFND
                 PI: Fund Number Account Number

Step B: Existing Case:

- Is the existing case resolved?

   If **YES**:   Attach Routing Slip to correspondence
                   and forward to Operator (Rep).

   If **NO**:   (see back)

Customer Service Administration Technical Training Department
PegaSHARES Gatekeeper Course, Job Aid

Making the headings larger and bolder is always an easy way to add contrast. Here a bold sans serif typeface does the trick, and the heading doesn't need to be underlined.

A hanging indent, plus more space between a bullet and the word that follows it, and between bullet items, makes the page more inviting and easier to read.

Using the paragraph space before/after feature to adjust the amount of space after paragraphs, instead of just using the return key, would allow you to create less or more space between bullet points than is shown here.

Software
WordPerfect
Title
Helvetica Bold 24 pt.
Text
Times 13 pt.
Headings
Helvetica Bold 14 pt.
Footer
Times 10 pt.
Page size
8 1/2" x 11"

Example 11

This page is from a user guide for a consumer product. It is used in training customer service employees, salespeople, and dental professionals.

2. using sonicare

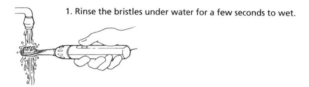

1. Rinse the bristles under water for a few seconds to wet.

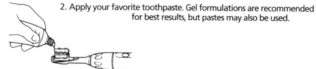

2. Apply your favorite toothpaste. Gel formulations are recommended for best results, but pastes may also be used.

3. To avoid splashing, put the brush in your mouth first, then press the power button.

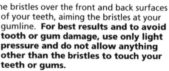

4. **Slowly** glide the bristles over the front and back surfaces of your teeth, aiming the bristles at your gumline. **For best results and to avoid tooth or gum damage, use only light pressure and do not allow anything other than the bristles to touch your teeth or gums.**

8

Plenty of white space, small blocks of text, and clear, simple illustrations make this page look unintimidating to the user.

Notice that the bold type in step 4 is a strong, heavy black. It provides contrast, and the reader is not likely to miss this important part of the instructions.

Software
PageMaker
Graphics
Drawings scanned into document
Title
Frutiger Black 16 pt.; number is 12 pt.
Text
Frutiger 10 pt.; bold type in step 4 is Frutiger Black 10 pt.
Page number
Frutiger Bold 7 pt.
Page size
6" x 7 1/2"

III

Appendixes

Page Planning Checklist

Use this list to plan your page layout. Adapt it to your needs.

Page size

- ❏ 8 1/2 x 11
- ❏ Other_____

Page orientation

- ❏ Vertical (portrait)
- ❏ Horizontal (landscape)

Printing

- ❏ Single-sided
- ❏ Double-sided

Additional notes

Layout

❏ 1   ❏ 2   ❏ 3   Column width_____

Space between columns_____

Margins (1/2 in. minimum; 3/4 in. minimum if bound)

Inside_____   Outside_____

Top_____   Bottom_____

Body (main) text

Typeface_____ _____ pt

Leading/line spacing_____

Chapter/section titles

Typeface_____ _____ pt

Headings

Level 1: Typeface_____ _____ pt

Level 2: Typeface_____ _____ pt

Level 3: Typeface_____ _____ pt

Header

Typeface_____ _____ pt

Footer

Typeface_____ _____ pt

Page number   ❏ In header   ❏ In footer

Typeface_____ _____ pt

Tables

_____

Graphics

_____

Tip: As a quick way of trying different looks, sketch layout ideas with paper and pencil.

✔ Consistency Checklist

Checking for consistency requires attention to detail. Check the following to make the format of a document consistent throughout.

Body (main) text

- ❑ Margins
- ❑ Typeface and point size
- ❑ Leading/line spacing
- ❑ Space between paragraphs

Chapter/section titles

- ❑ Typeface and point size
- ❑ Capitalization
- ❑ Alignment
- ❑ Space before and after

Headings

- ❑ Typeface and point size
- ❑ Capitalization
- ❑ Alignment
- ❑ Space before and after

Headers/footers

- ❑ Typeface and point size
- ❑ Alignment

Page numbers

- ❑ Typeface and point size
- ❑ Alignment

Tables

- ❑ Titles
- ❑ Text
- ❑ Indents
- ❑ Borders
- ❑ Alignment
- ❑ Space before and after

Lists

- ❑ Typeface and point size
- ❑ Indents
- ❑ Space between bullet/number and adjacent text
- ❑ Leading/line spacing

Columns

- ❑ Width
- ❑ Space between columns

Lines (rules)

- ❑ Weight
- ❑ Length
- ❑ Alignment
- ❑ Space before and after

Boxes

- ❑ Borders
- ❑ Alignment
- ❑ Space inside and outside

Shading (grayscale)

- ❑ Percentages
- ❑ Width/height of shaded areas
- ❑ Alignment

Graphics

- ❑ Size
- ❑ Alignment
- ❑ Space before and after

Captions/labels/callouts

- ❑ Typeface and point size
- ❑ Alignment

DESIGNING FOR A GLOBAL AUDIENCE

If your materials will be translated from English into another language, take the following into account as you design your pages.

- **Space.** Text is likely to take up at least 30 percent more space when it is translated from English. Prepare for this by leaving extra space on the page or using a larger point size in the English version. This may allow the translation to fit into the same amount of space.

  To avoid having to redraw or resize graphics, leave extra space for the translated text of callouts and labels.

- **Paper size.** Find out whether the translated version will be printed on the same size paper you're using for the English version.

- **Left/right orientation.** If an audience does not read from left to right, the layout of text as well as flow charts and any graphics that are meant to be read sequentially will need to be reoriented for these readers. Use arrows to indicate direction readers should follow.

- **Graphics.** Maximize the use of graphics to help readers understand information quickly and to reduce translation costs (pictures usually don't have to be translated).

  - Step-by-step instructions can often be conveyed entirely in a visual format, without words. Such visuals work best for explaining simple physical actions such as how to replace a printer cartridge or unpack a carton.

  - Use simple, generalized visuals; detailed or realistic images can be unfamiliar to readers and confuse them.

  - If you must show images of people, use simple silhouettes, line drawings, cartoons, or stick figures that do not indicate gender or race.

– Symbols readily understood by American audiences may be unfamiliar or have a completely different meaning to people in other cultures. Symbols showing hand gestures are especially likely to be misinterpreted. Make sure you understand how your audience is likely to interpret the symbols you plan to use.

If your international audience speaks English and will use an English version of your materials, pay attention to language as well as graphics:

- Avoid abbreviations.

- Avoid "Americanisms" such as colloquial terms and references to topics such as football or American foods.

- Use concrete verbs and nouns in short, simple sentences.

See William Horton's book, *Illustrating Computer Documentation*, listed in Appendix D, for more information on the special needs of global audiences.

BIBLIOGRAPHY AND RESOURCES

The first group of books listed below will be of special interest to training professionals. If you design non-training publications such as newsletters or brochures, or have a special interest in page layout, the graphic design books listed will provide you with dozens of examples and a detailed discussion of graphic design principles.

Training-related books

Horton, William. **The Icon Book: Visual Symbols for Computer Systems and Documentation**. John Wiley & Sons, Inc., New York, NY, 1994.

Horton, William. **Illustrating Computer Documentation: The Art of Presenting Information Graphically on Paper and Online**. John Wiley & Sons, Inc., New York, NY, 1991.

Kearny, Lynn. **Get Graphic! How to Make Visuals That Work**. Lynn Kearny, Oakland, CA, 1995. Available only from Lynn Kearny, 5379 Broadway, Oakland, CA 94618. Phone: 510-547-1896.

Misanchuk, Earl R. **Preparing Instructional Text: Document Design Using Desktop Publishing**. Educational Technology Publications, Englewood Cliffs, NJ, 1992.

Wileman, Ralph E. **Visual Communicating**. Educational Technology Publications, Englewood Cliffs, NJ, 1993.

Graphic design books

Gosney, Michael; Odam, John; Benson, Jim. **The Gray Book: Designing in Black and White on Your Computer**. Ventana Press, Chapel Hill, NC, 1990.

Koren, Leonard, and Meckler, R. Wippo. **Graphic Design Cookbook: Mix and Match Recipes for Faster, Better Layouts**. Chronicle Books, San Francisco, CA, 1989.

Modley, Rudolf. **Handbook of Pictorial Symbols: 3250 Examples From International Sources**. Dover Publications, Inc., Mineola, NY, 1976.

Moore, Kristine. **Desktop Publishing Design**. Mavis & Moore, Ann Arbor, MI, 1992. Available only from Mavis & Moore, 1706 Cambridge Rd., Ann Arbor, MI 48104-3647. Phone: 313-761-5210.

Parker, Roger C. **Looking Good in Print: A Guide to Basic Design for Desktop Publishing**; Ventana Press, Inc., Chapel Hill, NC, 1988.

Parker, Roger C. **The Makeover Book: 101 Design Solutions for Desktop Publishing**. Ventana Press, Inc., Chapel Hill, NC, 1989.

White, Jan V. **Graphic Design for the Electronic Age**. Watson-Guptill Publications, New York, NY, 1988.

White, Jan V. **Graphic Idea Notebook**. Watson-Guptill Publications, New York, NY, 1980.

White, Jan V. **Mastering Graphics**. R. R. Bowker Company, New York, NY, 1983.

Williams, Robin. **The Non-Designer's Design Book**. Peachpit Press, Inc., Berkeley, CA, 1994.

Magazines

Adobe Magazine
Adobe Systems Inc., 411 First Ave. S, Seattle, WA 98104-2871
206-628-2321

Before & After
1830 Sierra Gardens Dr., Suite 30, Roseville, CA 95661-2912
916-784-3880

Font & Function
Adobe Systems Inc., PO Box 7900, Mountain View, CA 94039-7900
800-866-6687

Publish
Integrated Media, Inc., 501 Second St., San Francisco, CA 94107
800-685-3435

Technique
10 Post Office Sq., Suite 600 South, Boston, MA 02109-4616
800-272-7377

Clip art and cartoons mentioned in this book

ClickArt clip art (see page 48)
T/Maker Company, 1390 Villa St., Mountain View, CA 94041
800-986-2537

Grantland cartoons (see page 49)
Available on disk or paper; updated regularly to include current workplace issues. Grantland Enterprises, Inc., 460 Bloomfield Ave., Suite 307, Montclair, NJ 07042
201-509-7688

Lynn Kearny graphic symbols (see page 48)
Available on disk or paper; custom-designed visuals for use in training materials and presentations. Lynn Kearny, 5379 Broadway, Oakland, CA 94618
510-597-1896

Megatoons by cartoonist Phil Frank (see page 49)
Available on disk or CD-ROM; updated regularly to include current workplace issues. Creative Media Services, PO Box 5955, Berkeley, CA 94705
800-358-2278

Mini Pics
Image Club Graphics Inc., c/o Publisher's Mail Service, 10545 W. Donges Ct., Milwaukee, WI 53224-9967
800-661-9410

Zedcor clip art (CD-ROM only) (see page 48)
Zedcor, Inc., 3420 North Dodge Blvd., Suite F, Tucson, AZ 85716
800-482-4567

Software mentioned in this book

Adobe Illustrator
Adobe Systems Inc., 411 First Ave. S, Seattle, WA 98104-2871
800-628-2320

Canvas
Deneba Software, 7400 SW 87th Ave., Miami, FL 33173
800-622-6827

CorelDRAW! (Windows only)
Corel Systems, 1600 Carling Ave., Suite 190, Ottawa ON K1Z8R7 Canada
800-772-6735

Excel
Microsoft Corp., One Microsoft Way, Redmond, WA 98052-6399
800-426-9400

Fontographer
Macromedia, 600 Townsend, San Francisco, CA 94103
800-288-8108

FrameMaker
Frame Technology Corp., 333 W. San Carlos St., San Jose, CA 95110
800-U4-FRAME

FreeHand
Macromedia, 600 Townsend, San Francisco, CA 94103
800-288-8108

Freelance Graphics (in Lotus NotesSuite)
Lotus Development Corp., Lotus North Office, 400 River Park Dr.,
North Reading, MA 01864
800-343-5414

MacDraw or **ClarisDraw** (Mac only)
Claris Corp., 5201 Patrick Henry Dr., Santa Clara, CA 95052
800-325-2747

Microsoft Word
Microsoft Corp., One Microsoft Way, Redmond, WA 98052-6399
800-426-9400

PageMaker
Adobe Systems Inc., 411 First Ave. S, Seattle, WA 98104-2871
800-628-2320

Persuasion
Adobe Systems Inc., 411 First Ave. S, Seattle, WA 98104-2871
800-628-2320

PowerPoint
Microsoft Corp., One Microsoft Way, Redmond, WA 98052-6399
800-426-9400

QuarkXPress
Quark, 1800 Grant St., Denver, CO 80203
800-788-7835

Ventura Publisher (Windows only)
Corel Systems, 1600 Carling Ave., Suite 190, Ottawa ON K1Z8R7
Canada
800-772-6735

WordPerfect
Novell Inc., 1555 No. Technology Way, Orem, UT 84057-2399
800-451-5151

CONTRIBUTORS

The following organizations and people contributed training materials shown in this book.

American Training Systems, page 100. Designed by Darlene Frank and Associates.

Bay Networks, Inc., page 78. Designed by Marty Murrillo.

The Dublin Group, Inc., page 86. Designed by Lance Dublin.

East Bay Municipal Utilities District, pages 68 and 69. Designed by Marna Owen & Associates.

Edify Corporation, page 103, designed by David Faust and Jean Mark; page 108, designed by David Faust and Max Ball.

Franklin Resources, Inc.

Hewlett-Packard, page 87. Designed by Christine Westall, Training Consultant, Americas Education.

International Center for Self-Governance, page 98. Designed by Kathy Indermill for the TESS Group.

James & Associates, page 101. Designed by Randolph James. Reprinted from *A No-Nonsense Pocket Guide to Common Sense Management*, 1991, James & Associates, Orangevale, CA.

Jane Ranshaw & Associates, Inc., page 84.

Kathleen Epperson, page 102.

Levi Strauss & Co., page 104. Designed by Brett Johnson.

Multimedia Training Newsletter. Brandon Hall, Ph.D., Editor and Publisher.

North American Mortgage Company, pages 106 and 107. Redesigned by Lee Alderman and Bonnie Brock.

Optiva Corporation, page 112. Designed by Chris Spivey, Tim Girvin Design, Inc.

Southwest Financial Systems, page 109. Designed by Darlene Frank and Associates.

Supercuts, Inc., pages 72 and 73.

The Synergy Group, pages 76 and 77. Designed by Thomas Leal.

The Training Alliance, Inc., page 90. Designed by Dawn Zintel.

Wells Fargo Bank.

Darlene Frank and Associates contributed examples not otherwise credited.

GLOSSARY

alignment	lining up the edges of the elements on a page
ascender	the part of a letter that extends above the main body of the letter
bleed	an element printed to the edge of the page
blend	see **graduated fill**
body text	the main text on a page; does not include headings and titles; also called *body type*
bullet	dot, square, or other symbol used to set off items on a list
CBT	acronym for computer-based training
CD-ROM	computer data on a compact disk; the disk can be read only, not written to
character	an individual letter, number, punctuation mark, or space in a typeface
clip art	copyright-free graphics available on floppy disk or CD-ROM, or from an online source
condensed type	type that has been made narrower
consistency	repeating elements in the same way throughout a document
contrast	juxtaposing elements that are very different, such as large and small or black and white
curly quotes	quotation marks printed in typeset-quality form (like "this"), not straight up and down (like "this"); also called *typographers' quotes* or, in some software programs, *smart quotes*
descender	the part of a letter that extends below the main body of the letter
dingbat	small, ornamental type characters; Zapf Dingbats is the most common
drop shadow	a solid or shaded box behind a lighter box
em dash	a long dash (—)
en dash	a short dash (–) that is one half the width of an em dash but wider than a hyphen
expanded type	type that has been widened
fill	shading or pattern used to fill a defined area such as a box
flush left	see **left aligned type**

font	a complete set of characters in a specific type style and size, such as Helvetica Bold 12 point
gradient	see **graduated fill**
graduated fill	a fill that goes from light to dark
grayscale	see **shading**
hairline	the thinnest line (1/4 point)
handouts	materials distributed to the audience in a presentation, workshop, or seminar
hanging indent	text in which each line after the first is indented
icon	visual symbol used to represent a concept or object
illustration software	program for creating illustrations and graphics
imagesetter	a high-resolution printer, like the Linotronic, used by commercial print services
instructor guide	written instructions for the person who will teach a class or work-shop; also called *leader's guide*
job aid	reference tool such as a summary or checklist, designed to provide information quickly
justified type	type that is aligned along both the left and right edges
kerning	adjusting the space between individual type characters
landscape	a page oriented in the horizontal, or wide, direction
leader's guide	see **instructor guide**
leading	the space between lines of type, measured in points; also called *line spacing*
left aligned type	type that is aligned along the left edge, with the right edge uneven; also called *flush left, ragged right*, or *unjustified*
legend	list or table explaining the symbols appearing on a graph or chart
legibility	the ease with which letters and words can be recognized; different from readability, which refers to the ease with which text can be read
line length	in typographic terms, refers to the length of a line of type
line spacing	the space between lines of type; see also **leading**
line weight	thickness of a line, measured in points
main text	see **body text**
normal type	type that is not bold or italics; also called *Roman*

page layout software	program for designing pages; provides more features and more control over layout and design than a word processing program
paragraph spacing feature	a feature in a word processing or page layout program that allows you to set the amount of space before and after a paragraph
pictograph	a graph that uses symbols to represent data
picture font	a font that consists of symbols instead of letters of the alphabet; also called *symbol font*
point	basic unit of measure for type
portrait	a page oriented in the vertical, or tall, direction
presentation software	program for creating slides, overhead transparencies, charts, and graphs
progress check	a short quiz designed to test what learners have learned up to that point; typically used after each section or at key points in a workbook
proximity	the visual grouping of related elements so that a page looks organized and readers can see the relationship between elements at a glance
pull quote	words set off from the main text on a page, usually in a different type style and point size, to make them prominent
ragged right	type with an uneven right margin
readability	the ease with which text can be read; different from legibility, which refers to the ease with which type can be recognized
repetition	deliberately repeating a graphic design element to add visual interest to pages and to help unify a document
reverse type	white type on a black background
right aligned type	type that is aligned along the right edge, with the left edge uneven
rule	the graphic design term for a line
sans serif	type without serifs
screen	see **shading**
screen shot	image of a computer screen, printed as a graphic on the page; also called *screen capture*
script	a category of type that looks like handwritten
self-paced workbook	a workbook designed to be used by learners studying on their own without an instructor
serif	a small stroke at the edges of type characters

shading	a pattern of small dots that can be printed in shades ranging from light gray to solid black; also referred to as *fill*, *grayscale*, or *screen*
sidebar	auxiliary text set aside from the main text on a page, often in a box
small caps	capital letters that are about the same size as lowercase letters
smart quotes	see **curly quotes**
straight quotes	quotation marks that are printed straight up and down, as they were on typewriters (like "this")
symbol font	see **picture font**
type family	all variations (including all sizes, weights, normal, bold, and italic versions) of the same typeface
type	see **typeface**
type style	a variation of a typeface, such as boldface or italics
typeface	a particular design of type that has a name, such as Helvetica
unjustified type	see **left aligned type**
workbook	a booklet learners use to study a subject; usually includes exercises and quizzes or tests

INDEX

Glossary terms are not included in this index.

M

Macintosh computers, xiv
main text. *See* body text
margins
    minimum size, 115
    right aligned text in, 10
Megatoons cartoons, 49
memory to run software programs, xiv
minus sign, 26

N

normal type, 22
number of
    boxes per page, 34
    characters per line, 19, 88
    point sizes per document, 17
    point sizes per page, 17
    shading percentages per page, 40
    text lines on overheads and slides, 88
    typefaces per document, 16
    typefaces per page, 16
numbers
    big and bold, 6
    as graphics, 6, 61, 62
    hyphenation of, 26
    on overheads and slides, 88
    use of tabs, 20

O

online clip art, xiv
outline lettering, 15
overhead transparencies, xiv, 79, 86-88

P

page design *See also* pages
    copying layouts, xv
    creating your own, xv, xvi
    planning, 115
page layout. *See* page design
page layout programs, xiv
page layout programs, using for
    borders, 34
    expanding and condensing type, 24
    leading, 18
    numbers in list, 62
    page numbers, 61
    paragraph spacing, 8
    rotated square, 58

    shadow box, 34
    underlines, 22
    wrapping text, 59
page numbers as graphics, 6, 61
page planning checklist, 115
pages. *See also* page design
    become pictures, 12
    enhanced dramatically, 16
    extra space at bottom of, 55
    organized, 7, 8, 9, 12
    planning, 115
    pretty, xvi
    viewing distance, 17
paper, 15, 17, 25, 79, 117
paragraph spacing feature, 8
paragraphs
    indenting, 20
    short, 7
people graphics 48, 117
pictographs, 51, 53
picture fonts, 60
pictures formed by information, xii, 12
pie charts, 51, 53
placement
    of captions, 56
    of graphics, 55
planning a page, 115
point size, 14, 16, 19, 22, 56, 60
    of lines, 28
    on overheads and slides, 88
    rules of thumb, 17
    in translations, 117
portrait page, 115
presentation software, xiv, 88
printing
    graphics, 46
    icons and symbols, 47
printing process, xv, 15, 39-40, 44, 54
printing resolution, 39-40
printing service, 39-40
professional typeset look, 26
proportion, pleasing, 55
proximity, 3, 7-8, 9, 12
pull quote, 31
punctuation at end of sentence, 26

Q

quick reference cards 99, 104, 109
quotation marks, 26

About the author

Darlene Frank is a training consultant, writer, and editor whose work has won awards from the International Society for Performance Improvement and the Society for Technical Communication. She is also the author of *Silicon English: Business Writing Tools for the Computer Age.* Her company, Darlene Frank and Associates, has been developing training materials for business and government organizations since 1979.

About this book

This book was produced in PageMaker 5.0 on a Macintosh IIvx. The body text is Palatino; headings are Helvetica. Most graphics were created in FreeHand; most contributor examples were scanned into the document. Final pages were printed on a 600 dpi laser printer; the book was printed from these camera-ready pages.

Would you like to contribute to the next edition of this book? If so, please send examples of page layouts you have designed to:

Darlene Frank and Associates
143 Moffitt St.
San Francisco, CA 94131

Please include your name, address, and phone number so we can contact you if we'd like to use your example. Thanks very much.

Your comments on this book are welcome. You can reach the author via e-mail at dfwrite@aol.com.

50 CASE STUDIES FOR MANAGEMENT AND SUPERVISORY TRAINING

Dr. Alan B. Clardy

Managers and supervisors will sharpen their analytical and decision-making skills with this new collection of fully reproducible case studies. Based on actual, real-life situations, these exercises prepare supervisors and team leaders for the challenging problems they face in today's complex workplace.

Training Objectives
- Improve participant's listening skills
- Empower employees to negotiate solutions fairly
- Provide opportunities for participants to practice new skills in a supportive environment
- Illustrate the skills needed to respond productively to complex issues

Activities Cover
- Performance appraisal
- Sexual harassment/ discrimination
- Coaching/counseling employees
- Managing effectively
- Managing disruptive employees
- Hiring the right person

Training Method
Case studies provide a forum for productive discussion and debate on sensitive issues. This book covers a full range of important management and supervisory concerns.

Each case study includes:
- Summary of the case
- Discussion questions which evoke thought and analysis
- Suggested solutions to the problems presented

Time Guidelines
- Each case study takes between 15 minutes and 1 hour.

3-Ring Binder	400 Pages	$89.95	Code ... 50MST
Paperback	400 Pages	$39.95	Code ... 50CSP

CHANGING PACE
Outdoor Games for Experiential Learning
Carmine M. Consalvo

This new collection of experiential activities in game format will enable trainers and facilitators to make effective use of the outdoors as a vehicle for learning. It contains sixty-three creative games that can be conducted easily and safely with a minimum of materials and preparation. Many of the activities can be run equally well indoors.

Each activity is presented in a standard format that includes a summary, a statement of objectives, a note of any materials required, time requirements, and detailed guidance on the effective use of the games in training. The games vary in length from a few minutes to over an hour. Together they provide a rich store of adventure, energy, and memorable learning.

Games Teach
- Cooperation
- Decision making
- Ethics
- Goal-setting
- Planning
- Rewards
- Trust
- Inter-team collaboration
- Creativity
- Energizers
- Evaluations
- Leadership
- Problem solving
- Risk taking
- Team learning
- Communication

200 Pages	Paperback	$34.95	Code ... CP

About the Author
Carmine M. Consalvo is a training consultant and president of WorkPlay, Inc. which he founded in 1984 to train professionals in the importance of humor, creativity, paradox, teamwork, and experiential training. He is also the author of the best-selling *Experiential Training Activities for Outside and In* and *Team Building Blocks* (both are available from HRD Press).

360° FEEDBACK

Strategies, Tactics, and Techniques for Developing Leaders

John E. Jones, Ph.D. & William L. Bearley, Ed.D.

Find out how the emerging technology of multi-source assessment and feedback (360° feedback) can benefit your organization. This handbook presents concrete methods for creating, adapting, and using survey methods to provide sharply targeted feedback to leaders. It contains case examples of applications of 360° feedback and spells out steps for creating instruments, analyzing data from them, and providing feedback in ways that both inform and inspire. The authors give step-by-step methods for using the best practices and avoiding the many pitfalls of 360° assessment and feedback.

Selected Contents

1. 360° Feedback as a System Intervention
2. 360° Feedback in Team Building
3. Assessing Training Needs with 360° Surveys
4. Assessing Outcomes of Training Investments
5. Creating Instruments for 360° Feedback
6. Data Analysis and Reporting
7. Getting Started in 360° Feedback
8. Appendices: Sample Worksheets, Survey Instruments, and Feedback Reports

200 Pages   Paperback $29.95
Order Code ... 360DF

ACCELERATED LEARNING RESOURCE KIT

Tim Maples

This book and video program clearly present the theory and practice of a variety of dramatically effective new training and learning techniques called Accelerated Learning. You will see how to deliver programs that: shorten learning time, help participants more effectively internalize new information, and make learning more self-directed, experiential, and enjoyable. Stimulating new presentation methods such as guided imagery, mind maps, individualized learning styles, active energizers, and using music to enhance learning are introduced through easy-to-implement, practical examples.

The book and resource kit include more than twenty powerful new techniques that you can use to put the principles of accelerated learning to work in your training.

Direct Benefits of Accelerated Learning

- Increased long-term retention and recall
- Increased speed and quality of learning
- Changed attitudes toward learning
- Greater productivity through increased motivation and accuracy of work performance

Resource Kit Includes

- 140-page Manual
- 1 video containing an overview, links, interviews, and real life examples
- 4 audio cassettes of musical selections to enhance learning, creativity, and visualization

Contents

Introduction
Brain Theory
Relaxed Alertness
Orchestrated Immersion
Active Processing
Roles of the Facilitator
Benefits of Accelerated Learning
List of Resources

$249.95   Order Code ... ALRK

The Only Annual That Gives You Disks for Easy Customization and Clean Reproductions.

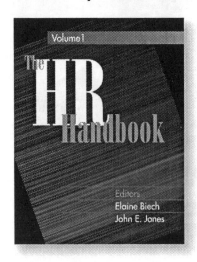

The HR Handbook
Edited by Elaine Biech & John E. Jones

Wouldn't you love to have access to the "tricks of the trade" used by the HR world's preeminent practitioners? In this inaugural edition of the HR Handbook, noted authorities such as Julie O'Mara, Dr. Arthur B. Van Gundy, Ron Galbraith, Scott Parry, and Donald Kirkpatrick share their best resources. You'll find over 50 exciting icebreakers, practical instruments, and helpful articles that will dramatically improve your next training session or presentation. And you can reproduce the materials without special copyright approval, which makes this handbook a great value for your training dollar.

WITH THE HR HANDBOOK YOU WILL:

- *Save Time*—All material is copyright-free. You can use it without special permission
- *Save Money*—Handouts, transparency masters, instruments are all ready-to-use. There's no need to invest in design or development
- *Enhance Your Professional Image*—The diskette allows you to customize and personalize the materials for your audience, ensuring a coordinated "look"
- *Be a Smashing Success*—All activities have been designed by experienced professionals and have been field-tested with numerous audiences for guaranteed success

Contents

Icebreakers and Energizers
  Interactive Name Tents
  Prioritizing: Make It All Fit
  Rainbow Connections
  Your Learning Language
Learning Activities and Games
  Eggspectable
  PBJ Management: From the Kitchen to the Workplace
  Power Circle
  The Hats We Wear
  Opposing Solutions: An Exercise in Conflict Management
  Win a Few, Lose a Few!
  The Track Layers: A Team Problem Solving Activity
  Peak Performance
  Career Development Camera
  How Personal Vision Fits Into a Learning Organization
  What Drives You Crazy
  Diversity Dialogues
  Opening Windows: Polishing Communication Skills
  Air Cliche
  Building Quality In
  Leadership for Change—What to Work on First
  Sexual Harassment: The Gray Areas
  Change Management
  Creating a Collaborative Workplace
Role Plays, Case Studies, and Critical Incidents
  Meeting Management
  Natura
  Paul Blaczyk
  Foster Cooperation
Assessment and Feedback Instruments
  Multicultural Communication Self Assessment
  Analytical Thinking Test
  Perseverance: Value Preference Inventory and General Beliefs Inventory
  Assessing Where the Team Is: A Checklist
  Teamness Perception Survey
  Beliefs About Leadership

Models for Development
  Achieving Balance in Your Life
  Keep it Simple Problem Solving
  Three Essential Process Tools for Teams
  Mind Webs: Tapping the Group Mind
  Staff Meetings: A Shared Model for Increased Efficiency and Energy
  White Men and Diversity: Why Men Are the Way They Are
  Post-Heroic Leadership: From Hierarchy to Role Set
  Four More Ways to Manage Conflict
  Effective Change Management
Strategies and Techniques
  15 Ideas for the First 15 Minutes of Class
  Let's Celebrate!
  Positive Reinforcement
  Flic Clips
  What Do You Want Them to Learn?
  New-Manager Assimilation
  The Diversity Initiative Requires Planning and Business Discipline
  The Exciting Shift from Authoritarian to Collaborative Power: Questions to Ask Ourselves as Consultants and Trainers
  The New World of Work
  Clearing the Air
  Across the Great Divide: A Method for Mediating Differences
  Fools Rush In: Intervening in Interpersonal Conflict Situations
  Spirituality in the Workplace
  Large-Group System-Wide Change Technology
  Mega Planning: A Framework for Integrating Strategic Planning, Needs Assessment, Quality Management, Benchmarking, and Reengineering

3-Ring Binder with Diskette	$89.95	**Code … HHM**
(Diskette comes in Microsoft Word 7.0 format)		
Paperback	$59.95	**Code … HH**